T0068131

I'm
Not an
Addict

...I'm
Just an
Ass!

I'd Rather Be a Smart Ass
Than a Dumb Ass!

Geri Petito

ARCHWAY
PUBLISHING

Copyright © 2016 Geri Petito.

All rights reserved. No part of this book may be used or reproduced by any means, graphic, electronic, or mechanical, including photocopying, recording, taping or by any information storage retrieval system without the written permission of the author except in the case of brief quotations embodied in critical articles and reviews.

Archway Publishing books may be ordered through booksellers or by contacting:

Archway Publishing
1663 Liberty Drive
Bloomington, IN 47403
www.archwaypublishing.com
844-669-3957

Because of the dynamic nature of the Internet, any web addresses or links contained in this book may have changed since publication and may no longer be valid. The views expressed in this work are solely those of the author and do not necessarily reflect the views of the publisher, and the publisher hereby disclaims any responsibility for them.

Any people depicted in stock imagery provided by Thinkstock are models, and such images are being used for illustrative purposes only. Certain stock imagery © Thinkstock.

ISBN: 978-1-4808-3042-4 (sc)
ISBN: 978-1-4808-3043-1 (e)

Library of Congress Control Number: 2016906184

Print information available on the last page.

Archway Publishing rev. date: 10/14/2020

This book is dedicated to

my daughter, Tiffany, and my
grandchildren, Christian and Aria.

You are the loves of my life.

May God bless you, and may you never find yourself

struggling with an addiction.

All my love,

"MeMom"

Contents

Acknowledgments ix

Preface xiii

Introduction xv

P.I.S.S. O.F.F. xvii

The Jackass Test xxi

The New ~~12~~ 13 Steps xxiii

According to Geri xxiii

Honesty 1

Faith 9

Surrender 16

Soul-Searching 21

Integrity 26

Acceptance 31

Humility 36

Willingness 44

Forgiveness 49

Maintenance 54

Making Contact 58

Service 62

Put Down The Gun 66

Change: Your Choice 71

"2020" 74

Divine Intervention 84

My Story 90

"Niacin" 117

"Saved By Grace" 125

"My Book Aint For Wimps" 169

"MsNiteOwl Poker" 185

Amazing Book Reviews 237

Acknowledgments

I want to thank my brother, Anthony, for being the most supportive and amazing brother a girl could ask for. Your selfless actions for your family go above and beyond all expectations. Thank you for always being there when I most needed you. I can never repay you.

I also want to thank Andrea Giordano for her contribution to the writing of this book and for giving me some great input. It was amazing collaborating with her. If it wasn't for her taking my handwritten, scribbled notebook and my pieces of scrap paper and putting my ideas into book form, this book may still be just a dream. I also want to thank her for her computer knowledge, for knocking down doors, and for moving mountains so that this book could be in the market to help others.

For my cousin Michael (a.k.a. Mook), for such a young man at the time, you became one of my rocks. I thank God for you. Every day I look at your poem, that hangs so graciously on my wall. "The friend I found in you". That title is an understatement. God, has graced me not only with a loving and supportive cousin, but more so with "the friend I found in *you*"!

Last, but certainly not least, I want to thank my gracious father. Thank you, Dad, for not giving up on me. You stood by my side and taught me my values. I know that, due to your Alzheimer's, you will never understand that this book is being published and that I am helping others as you have helped me your whole life. I know you are in there, Dad, and I pray you have a glimmer of memory for the love I have for you. I love you, Dad.

Love, Geri

I would like to thank Geri Petito for so many things, but most of all for saving me. For giving me the strength and encouragement to leave an abusive relationship to a drug addict and for guiding me to know my self-worth. To say you are a friend is an understatement. You are so much more to me, and you have so much to offer others. You touch so many lives, and I am blessed and proud to call you my friend. I look forward to our future collaborations and to our ever-growing friendship. You are a remarkable woman. I love you.

Andrea

I would like to thank Jusella Bella for her contribution in revising my book. This revision took place the beginning of 2020, four years after the original book. I couldn't have done this without her help and support, I met Jusella Because of my book being published and we remained friends since.

I would also like to thank Suzette Lucas a childhood friend who came to my aide less than an hour notice to take my cover photo and send it to Archway Publishing. Lucas Photography Saved the day "I love you Suzette"

Last but not least, A special thank you to Kell Ramos for writing, singing & producing "The Geri Petito Show Jingle".

Preface

*"I'm not an addict, this too shall pass. I'm
not an addict, I'm just an ass."*

Twenty five years ago, on July 27, 1991, *I* made a decision to stop using drugs. *I* was what you might call a
functioning drug addict. My own family never knew *I*
used, and most of my friends had no clue either. But
then that day came when *I* knew *I* was becoming out
of control. So, *I* checked myself into a rehab facility
and stayed there for the full thirty days. It changed my
life—or, I should say, *I changed my life!* *I* have been
clean and sober ever since, but not just physically; *I*
have been clean and sober mentally as well.

Yes, my friend, mental sobriety is a real thing. It
involves making sound, thoughtful choices. For example,
I chose not to be a dry drunk! You know the kind:
sober but miserable, sober yet thinking of picking up,
sober but fighting it 24/7 . . . until you can't fight it
anymore. *I* chose to live a life that involved never thinking of picking up again, and *I* chose to live a happy,
productive, sober life. Now I'm here to tell you that
those things are possible for you, too!

I no longer consider myself **"a recovering addict."** I can't even count how many friends and family

members have passed away from addiction over the past twenty-five years. I ask myself over and over again, "If I could do it, why couldn't they?"

I made a decision to find the answers to achieving an obtainable path to recovery. It took many years, but *I* am finally ready to disclose what *I* believe to be the answer. The new 13 steps to recovery according to Geri.

Introduction

This book is not intended to minimize the importance of your support system, whether it's a group meeting, a sponsor, your church, your family, or your friends. Instead, the goal of this book is to bring a greater awareness to the real problem. Which is *"YOU AND YOUR CHOICES"! YOU, YOU, YOU! Not* people, places or things. Not constantly making excuses for "your" disease of addiction. All diseases are curable. YUP! That's right!

I decided to share with you what has helped me change my life. I changed my thinking from unhealthy to healthy. I decided to put the blame of my unhealthy choices on *ME!* We all have scars, yes we *all* do. Some worse than others. But **we all** have the power to heal them. Emotional scars heal. I promise!

Remember growing up and how you got scrapes, bruises, broken bones, broken hearts and yet they all seemed to heal. Do you want to live a miserable life? End up losing your life? Or, do you want to live a long healthy happy life. *You* have the power to choose!

P.I.S.S. O.F.F.

This book is intended to P.I.S.S O.F.F. a lot of people, but don't worry—that's a good thing! P.I.S.S O.F.F. means to:

P Possibly
I Infiltrate
S Sensible
S Solutions
O Offering
F Favorable
F Fundamentals

I'm sure that by now you want to tell me to kiss off, but, as you may have heard, *kiss* can actually mean K.I.S.S.—"Keep it simple, stupid." I, however, have my own take on what K.I.S.S. means:

K Keeping
I Ideas
S Safe and
S Sound

Ultimately, your goal is to C.H.A.N.G.E. How so? Well, I'm glad you asked. You will C.H.A.N.G.E. by:

C Channeling
H Healthy
A Amazing
N New
G Grounded
E Endeavors

Before we start going through the steps involved with your transformation, I want to touch on the "science" of addiction. Don't worry, I'm not going to bore or confuse you. While going through my own process, I said, "I'm going to K.I.S.S it ("keep it simple, stupid") for myself so that I can understand everything and not lose my focus."

So, let's start by acknowledging that your addiction is *not* a disease. It's your *choice*. There are so many articles, professionals, and self-help groups that will debate this issue until everyone's blue in the face, but think about it: A disease is something you get. You *get* cancer. You *get* Alzheimer's. You don't ever say, "I'm going to choose to have a brain tumor today," do you? No, you don't choose that, but you *do* choose to be an addict. There is a behavioral problem that leads to addiction.

Many support groups teach that addiction is a disease, but they also say that loved ones should stop helping the addict and show them "tough love" until he or she hits rock bottom. That never made sense to me. If my loved one had a disease, I would never close the door on them. There would be no such thing as hitting rock bottom. So, if this is indeed the recommended way of dealing with an addict, how can addiction be a disease? You don't wait for a cancer patient (who, as

I said, *does* have a disease) to hit rock bottom before helping him or her. Also, if you compare the brain of an addict and the brain of a nonaddict, you'll see that there's no scientific difference between them and that nothing indicates that the former is suffering from a disease.

Now, what you're doing by taking drugs and drinking alcohol is changing the chemical balance of your brain. Often, adding prescription medication like antidepressants and antianxiety pills to the mix causes additional harm due to the imbalance of serotonin and norepinephrine.

Studies have shown that when you do or think about something enough, the chemistry of your brain will change. Different areas of the brain will be more or less active depending on how much you use them, and that level of activity will become the normal state of your brain. But your brain can continue to change, depending on the kinds of thoughts you allow to dominate your thinking.

So, to break that down in my terms: When you have unhealthy thoughts, live an unhealthy lifestyle, surround yourself with unhealthy people, and live in an unhealthy environment, your mind-set will be unhealthy as a result. But once you start thinking healthy, acting healthy, and living healthy, you will have a healthy mind. Your brain will do all the hard work for you; all *you* have to do is feed it. Positive mind, positive life. As the saying goes, mind over matter.

The Jackass Test

1. Have you ever lied; stolen; compromised your principles; hocked something; abandoned someone; verbally or physically abused someone; put blame on someone; lost your home; spouse, kids, or job; forced yourself on someone; woken up naked in a random place; or thought of suicide?

   (If the answer is yes to any or all of the above, then your answer is yes to all of the following questions.)

2. Are you an ass?
3. Are you an ass?
4. Are you an ass?
5. Are you an ass?
6. Are you an ass?
7. Are you an ass?
8. Are you an ass?
9. Are you an ass?
10. Are you an ass?
11. Are you an ass?
12. Are you an ass?
13. **Yes, I'm as ass!**

The New ~~12~~ **13** Steps

According to Geri

1. Decide to stop lying to myself and others. Admit that I am *choosing* to allow my addiction to destroy lives, including my own.

2. Realize that I am an ass and that I need to find a power greater than myself.

3. Get down on my knees and cry out to God, "I am helpless without you."

4. Look in the mirror and hate what I see looking back at me. (Not to worry; step number ten's got this.)

5. Stop making excuses and blaming others for the horrible things I've done and instead decide to change my behavior.

6. Stand up tall and tell God, "I'm ready to go to war! I must fight to be right. Please show me how!"

7. Beg God for forgiveness and ask him to remove my crap!

8. Write down the name of every innocent victim who was affected by my addiction.

9. Get in touch with each victim, honestly and humbly take ownership of my behavior, and ask for forgiveness.

10. Look in the mirror every day and take full responsibility for all of my actions. That face looking back may soon start to like me.

11. Continue to talk to God every day, asking for encouragement, guidance, and forgiveness.

12. Realize I have to wake the "f" up and practice these principles on a daily basis while encouraging other addicts to do the same. I'm worth it, baby!

13. **If you feel like blowing your brains out by now, put the damn gun down! I promise, you won't regret it!**

Chapter 1

Honesty

Let's be honest
Once and for all
Stand on the truth
And you won't fall

I'm not an addict
This I know
Because my God
He tells me so

You see this world
Will hold you down
It lies and says
You can't be found

But God says, "Listen,
That's all such bull.
Your cup's not empty,
Your cup is full!"

The devil laughs
Right in your face
Makes you think
You're such a waste

It's up to you
To fight your fight
To let him know
He's wrong, not right!

You weren't born
To be this way
Screw the world
With what they say

I'm not an addict
This too shall pass
I'm not an addict
I'm just an ass!

Being honest with yourself is seemingly one of the hardest things to do. I'm not exactly sure why that is. Maybe it's because once you become honest, things become real. Once things become real, you have to be deal with them, and we all know what that can lead to.

Dealing with life can be very unpleasant at times. Feelings suck! Let's be honest: When you're forced to see the truth, it's easier to numb the difficult feelings that arise rather than let yourself experience them. Unfortunately, numbing your feelings leads to more of a mess. It leads you down a dark path filled with deception.

I remember getting my heart broken when I was young. That was one of the worst feelings ever. Soon after, I attended my first funeral. Ugh! As life went on, more and more painful things happened. Holy crap! I just wanted to run away.

For some of you reading this today, your first attempt at self-medication was probably something like sneaking a drink from your parents' bar or smoking pot with an older cousin. As you got older, you likely tried different drugs. You kept chasing after that truly euphoric experience—that rush, that high, that feeling you couldn't quite put into words. You abused alcohol, sex, gambling, or anything else that held you captive.

Maybe you were depressed and got antidepressants from your doctor, but you abused them after convincing yourself that the degree of your depression warranted it. You tricked yourself into thinking that what you were doing was fine because, after all, the pills were prescribed by a doctor.

We all know that "fine" and "good" aren't the same thing. A common mind-set is that taking too many prescription pills doesn't make you a "real" addict because the pills were given to you by a doctor in order to help you feel better, but is there really any difference between that kind of pill user and a person who has a drink to relax after a hard day's work? No. Any mood-altering substance is an unhealthy outlet.

While everyone needs an outlet in life, it's crucial to choose a healthy one rather than an unhealthy one. The key is to find something that doesn't cause a negative effect on your health, finances, job security, home life, social life, or daily activities. Things that *do* negatively affect those areas are temporary fixes. As long as you have your "happy kit," you'll feel like life is great. The problem, however, is that once you come down, life not only sucks again, but it's even worse than before because of all the horrible things you piled onto it while high.

There are all kinds of resources available to you if you're serious about getting better. I went into counseling years ago and continue to speak with someone one-on-one. I've stayed in touch with all my past counselors, who are now my friends and—get this—even ask *me* for advice! You need to be in some kind of counseling so that someone objective can help you look at your circumstances from a different perspective.

Women seem to have an easier time deciding to seek counseling than men do. We're used to opening up to our friends about our feelings on a daily basis while most men aren't. I get that, but if you don't muster up the guts to talk to someone then you can't heal.

Now, I want to talk about certain kinds of support groups and meetings. I'll never tell you not go to them, but I want to share why I stopped going. When I first got out of the rehab facility, I was told that I must find a sponsor and go to meetings every night. So, I did what I was told, and after three months I not only wanted to use again, I wanted to blow my brains out. Here I was, trying to stay clean, and yet I was told that I must go into a room with tons of other addicts so that we could all talk about our addictions. That didn't work for me. I'm an all-or-nothing kind of person, so I decided that if I truly wanted to stay clean, I needed to stop calling myself an addict. "Hi, I'm Geri. I'm an addict." Boo! Nope. I'm not!

I decided that God was the answer for me. I found a great church filled with recovering addicts like myself, but the difference was that we never talked about drugs, alcohol, or addiction. We focused on renewing ourselves, changing our bad habits to healthy ones, accepting forgiveness, and learning how to love our broken selves.

That worked for me. I dove into a healthy lifestyle filled with healthy outings, parties, movies, books, and more. I changed most of the people, places, and things in my life, and you need to do the same. Find a healthy outlet for you that doesn't make you think of picking up. I promise you, having such an outlet works. If meetings *do* work for you, that's great, but if you find yourself staying clean for only so long, then try doing it my way. It certainly can't hurt.

So, like I said, it's easy. You just need to:

1. Dive into counseling.

2. Find a great church (or support group).

3. Find healthy friends and a healthy group setting.

4. Get up early and make your bed every day. (I'll touch on this more in Chapter Twelve.)

5. Change your diet.

It's important that you understand that your diet is the key to your health. You need to get off all sugar, caffeine, soda (including diet), and processed food. I know it sounds overwhelming, but if you do this for thirty days, I promise that your cravings will be curbed. If you can do it for thirty days, then try it for sixty, then ninety, then—why stop? Once you consistently feed your cells healthy, nutritious food they stop craving harmful foods. They also tell your brain to stop craving whatever you were addicted to.

I took healthy eating to the extreme. I went away to learn about fasting for health. I dove into a mostly organic diet and also started using organic cleaning supplies, an organic mattress, organic bedding, and organic personal items and completely detoxed my body and continue to do so a couple of times a year. I started getting colonics a few times a year to clean out my intestines for health maintenance. I invested in a juicer and started drinking healthy green shakes daily. Health-food stores became my best friends.

I'm not saying you need to go to the extreme that I did, but removing a few of the "toxic" items from your diet to start will make a world of difference. Baby steps! One positive change will lead you to many more.

I bet you're thinking, "Damn, I can't afford to eat healthy." Hmm, that's funny. You were able to afford feeding your addiction for all those years. The difference between you and me is that I *chose* to spend my money on staying healthy and not on staying an addict.

I promise you: It works if you work it! Your *choice*!

Notes

_____

_____

_____

_____

_____

_____

_____

_____

_____

_____

_____

_____

_____

_____

_____

_____

_____

_____

_____

_____

_____

Notes

_____

_____

_____

_____

_____

_____

_____

_____

_____

_____

_____

_____

_____

_____

_____

_____

_____

_____

_____

_____

_____

Chapter 2

Faith

Put your faith
In something greater
Do it now
Don't wait till later

Lord, my God,
Please keep me sane
I need a switch
To shut off my brain

When I feel shattered, broken, and torn
When I ache and cry, tired and worn
You lift me up and wipe my tears
You whisper gently to have no fears

For my free will
Has lost control
To get it back
Will be my goal

I need to just
Have faith in you
There's nothing more
That I can do!

I'm not an addict
This too shall pass
I'm not an addict
I'm just an ass!

Where does your faith lie? Is it in yourself or in something greater? We all need someone to lean on—someone we can talk to, vent to, pour out our feelings to; someone to simply listen and tell us everything's going to be okay.

Many of us walk through life pretending to be so strong, pretending that we don't need anyone, but that's when we're at our weakest and in desperate need of help. Believe it or not, it takes a strong person to admit they need help. Weak people refuse to ask for help when they're drowning, and that's where God comes in. In order to *not* drown, you need to put your faith in him, not in yourself.

For me, growing up Catholic and going to Catholic school in New York was traumatic. When I was in seventh grade, my family moved to New Jersey, and I begged my parents to let me attend public school. Making that transition was the greatest sense of freedom I'd ever felt. Back then, things were very different. My brother once got whacked across the knuckles with a stack of rulers that were held together by rubber bands. (How about that? He was the "bad one" and I was the angel!) I'm not proud of this, but once my mom actually dragged a nun by her habit across the floor! Also, when I was in fifth grade, I told my girlfriend that my mom had let me see Elvis the previous night. Sister Metilda, who towered over me, tapped me on the shoulder and sternly said, "You are going to *hell* if you watch him." All I could think was, "Then hell must be a fun place!" No, seriously, that experience scared the crap out of me (and so did Sister Metilda).

In seventh grade, before I moved to New Jersey, I made my confirmation. My classmates and I were lined up; forced to enter a small, dark room with a window the size of a coaster; and told to kneel on a hard, wooden bench. As if that wasn't bad enough, a deep voice then came through the hole and said, "Yes, my child, tell me your sins." Huh? Was my dad behind that wall? I was forced to tell this headless stranger how "bad" I had been and then, based on how many "sins" I'd committed, was ordered to say a certain number of Hail Marys. I said them so fast—so that I could leave and go play—that I didn't even know what I was supposedly praying for while reciting them. I remember coming home and asking my mother, "Mommy, why do I have to tell that strange man I was bad? Can't I just tell God?" "Yup," she said.

That experience was the beginning of my realization that sometimes people maintain traditions they were brought up with out of guilt and a fear of offending their family. I, however, was too strong-willed to care about such things. If something didn't make sense, I couldn't believe in it. If I couldn't believe in it, I couldn't have anything to do with it. Guilt isn't a good reason to do something. It can hold us back from so much. Guilt makes you doubt yourself, and it can even make you hate yourself and feel worthless.

When I was a child in Catholic school, I chose to think outside the box because I didn't like the company inside it! As I got older and realized how much hypocrisy there was in churches, religions, and even recovery meetings, I discovered that so many people I'd trusted from those worlds ended up betraying me. I therefore decided that, other than my immediate family members and a few close friends—all of whom had always shown me unconditional love—my faith had to be put in God, my Heavenly Father. I committed my soul to my Lord Jesus Christ and stood on his word: "Jesus said to him, 'I am the way, and the truth, and the life; no one comes to the Father but through Me.'" (John 14:6)

Here's the thing, people: Everyone freaks out when they think about the work they have to do for their salvation. The idea becomes overwhelming, and often you'll throw up your hands and say, "God could never forgive me after all the horrible stuff I did." That's distorted thinking. Stop believing what you've been told by religion and by churches.

One of my favorite passage in the Bible is when Jesus says, "It is finished!" (John 19:30) Once I read that, I realized that God did all the work on the cross so that I could be forgiven. That means that the debt owed to Jesus's father was wiped away completely and forever; it was paid in full. Not that Jesus wiped away any debt that *he* owed his father, but rather that Jesus eliminated the debt owed by mankind—the debt of sin.

We're no longer bound to our sins, nor to the

guilt associated with those sins, as long as we move forward and make things right. Jesus knew more than two thousand years ago, before he accepted the cup for us, all the horrible sins we would commit, and yet he still said, "Yes, I will die for you. You are worth it." You see? So, the only "work" we need to do is to talk to God daily and ask him for the strength to continue uphill. If it worked for me, it will work for you, my friend. God is good *all* the time, and all the time, God is good. Your *choice*!

Notes

_____

_____

_____

_____

_____

_____

_____

_____

_____

_____

_____

_____

_____

_____

_____

_____

_____

_____

_____

_____

Notes

_____

_____

_____

_____

_____

_____

_____

_____

_____

_____

_____

_____

_____

_____

_____

_____

_____

_____

_____

_____

_____

_____

Chapter 3

Surrender

It's time to give up
This control that I show
To surrender my will
And just let it go

'Cause keeping control
The way that I've been
Is out of control
And I never win

I lie to myself
And say that I'm good
I don't have that power
The power I should

My diet is bad
It's hurting me so
Sugar and caffeine
I must let them go

So, God, here it is
I surrender to you
Take charge of my life
I don't have a clue

I'm not an addict
This too shall pass
I'm not an addict
I'm just an ass!

How many times have you felt the urge to give up on life? Probably more times than you care to remember. Instead of thinking with the mind-set of giving up, think with the mind-set of "surrendering up." Surrender up all your unhealthy thoughts and habits to God, and ask God to help you get rid of them once and for all. Here's the thing: God can't rid you of all your crap until you give him permission to do so. Until then, you are choosing to hold onto it. Do you get it, dumb-ass?

When I say you gotta give God permission to help you, what I mean is simple. We were all born with free will—with choices. I would hate to live a life without choices, a life where I was constantly forced to do things I didn't want to do. I thank God for that not being the case. So, God will back away as needed and let us continue to make our own choices, good or bad, until—you guessed it—we fall on our faces and finally need him.

Look at it this way: It's no different than a parent teaching his or her child tough love. That's the hardest thing for a parent to do, watching their child get hurt time and time again. It's gut-wrenching, but, deep down, a parent know it's best to let this happen until the child finally comes to him or her for help. That parent is waiting with open arms. It's no different with God. My earthly father has never failed me, and I can assure you that my Heavenly Father never has either! Your *choice*!

Notes

_____

_____

_____

_____

_____

_____

_____

_____

_____

_____

_____

_____

_____

_____

_____

_____

_____

_____

Notes

_____

_____

_____

_____

_____

_____

_____

_____

_____

_____

_____

_____

_____

_____

_____

_____

_____

_____

Chapter 4

Soul-Searching

To search my soul
Down deep inside
Reveal all things I used to hide

To bring them forth
For me to heal
Stop the lying
And make it real

The stuff I've hidden
Must now be shown
The crap I've done
Must all be known

So cut the crap
And make your list
It won't be easy
You'll get pissed

But if you want
To really heal
Get on your knees
Bow down and kneel

Cry out in pain
To wipe your slate
Relieve your shoulders
Of excess weight

I'm not an addict
This too shall pass
I'm not an addict
I'm just an ass

Unless you do some serious soul-searching—yes, *serious* soul-searching—you will never get over your addiction. You need to get honest with yourself once and for all. Stop putting blame elsewhere. Own it! You heard me—*own* it! Then and only then will you be able to heal. Yes, we all have issues and we all have sadness in our lives, but grow the "f" up and take full responsibility for your actions. If you do this, my friend, you can heal.

I once received some of the best advice of my life during a therapy session. My biggest issues always seemed to revolve around my "horrible" mother. We would argue, fight, and scream at each other on a daily basis. I hated her. She was just so mean-spirited! Ugh. I was always trying to figure out how I could change her.

Well, guess what? I couldn't! That's right—you can't change someone. The advice I was given in therapy was that I needed to stop worrying about changing the other person and instead change the way I *reacted* to that person. Eventually the person who's upsetting you will have no choice but to stop trying to push your buttons if you don't react to what he or she is doing. Doesn't that make sense? Once I was able to change my reaction to my mother, I was able to start letting go of my anger toward her.

The last thing I'll share about my mom is this: In time I came to understand her. Hurt people hurt people. My mom was abused as a child, so, once I let go of my own hurts, I was able to see hers. She was already deceased when I was finally able to forgive her, but at least I did. Now she's up there smiling and saying, "I accept your apology, my daughter." Again, that's no different than what God will do for you!

So, let go of your past, forgive those who hurt you, and take responsibility for your actions, because if you don't, you're no different than anyone who hurt you, and the cycle of doom continues. Break that cycle now! Your *choice*!

Notes

_____

_____

_____

_____

_____

_____

_____

_____

_____

_____

_____

_____

_____

_____

_____

_____

_____

_____

_____

_____

_____

Notes

_____

_____

_____

_____

_____

_____

_____

_____

_____

_____

_____

_____

_____

_____

_____

_____

_____

Chapter 5

Integrity

To have integrity
You must admit
To yourself and God
You are in a pit

Look in the mirror
Once and for all
The man in the glass
Will make you crawl

So admit your wrongs
And make them right
Turn your sins from black
To sparkling white

I'm not an addict
This too shall pass
I'm not an addict
I'm just an ass

It saddens me that integrity has become a lost art. A person's handshake used to mean something. A person's word was golden. In your own life, let your "yes" *be* your "yes," and let your "no" *be* your "no." That's the only way to get people to trust you again.

Your addiction destroyed your integrity, but I'm here to tell you that you can get it back. Trust me, I know. An important step in getting your integrity back is to stop making excuses for your behavior. *Stop!* I made a conscious decision to stop blaming anyone in my past that has ever hurt me, and I was able to put my addiction behind me once and for all and earn back the respect of myself and of others."

This section of this chapter applies to the ladies reading this. For me, growing up as a young girl who was very physically developed at a way too early age wasn't fun. I'm sure you can imagine stupid boys making stupid boob jokes. If that wasn't bad enough, when I was thirteen years old, a perverted, older, married man cornered me, put his hand down my shirt, whispered obscenities in my ear, and threatened to harm me if I ever told your dad. Well, as a result of my experiences, I grew up wanting to hide my body. How crazy! My trust issues with men skyrocketed, and all my romantic relationships crashed. Ladies, if you've ever been a victim of a man's abuse, I promise that you can heal just as I did. I refuse to allow anyone else's sin or garbage keep me in bondage.

I know of an amazing woman who was sexually molested by her father and forced to have sex with him well into her teens. She has not only recovered emotionally, through the Lord Jesus Christ, but she even ministered to her father on his deathbed. Can you image that? I don't think I would be capable of that.

But, surely, if she can heal from the worst fate a woman could ever imagine, you can, too.

Now, this section applies to the guys out there. Did you grow up watching your dad abuse or mistreat your mom, your sister, or another loved one? Are you following in his footsteps because of your addiction? Are you taking out your issues on your partner or your family? Well, now is the time to stop. Now is the time to break that cycle. It's in your hands. You *do not* have to be that person.

So, what do you think? Can you look in the mirror and say, "I'm ready to accept full responsibility for my actions. I will no longer blame others." Of course you can. Good job! Your *choice*!

Notes

Notes

_____

_____

_____

_____

_____

_____

_____

_____

_____

_____

_____

_____

_____

_____

_____

_____

_____

_____

_____

_____

Chapter 6

Acceptance

Acceptance starts within ourselves
I'm sure you heard that once before
Now listen up and make it known
Your body and mind must be restored

So please ask God
What you should do
Out with the old
In with the new

Remove my crap
Just pray to him
To make you see
What once was dim

I give it up
My junk to you
I need to see
A better view

I'm ready now
To make that change
I know to you
That might seem strange

But now it's time
Once and for all
To give it up
So not to fall

I'm not an addict
This too shall pass
I'm not an addict
I'm just an ass

It's time to accept the fact that you are not a mistake. God doesn't make mistakes. It's time to accept the good in yourself. Accept your flaws as part of being human. Accept your worth and believe in yourself. Only you have the power to do that. No one can do it for you. Look in the mirror and say to yourself, "I'm worth it!"

I finally realize my self-worth. I didn't want to be that selfish, lying, untrustworthy addict anymore, but I couldn't make my transformation without God's help. Today I know that he's here for me. I choose to wake up every day with a great attitude and a smile on my face. Life is good! If you're not there yet, remember the saying "Fake it till you make it!"

You see, your brain is an amazing thing. It can be your best friend or your worst enemy. Whatever you say to yourself, your brain will believe it to be true. It stores the information you provide it with, and then it releases a corresponding message to your body, turning on your fight-or-flight mechanism when it perceives there to be a crisis or threat of some kind. So, if you tell your brain that something very bad is happening, your brain will trigger the release of stress hormones—which will prime you to either fight or flee a scene if necessary—in order to aid in your survival. You see?

I've chosen to continuously feed my mind with happy, healthy, funny, warm, and fuzzy thoughts as much as possible. When there truly is something bad happening, my brain is healthy enough to allow me to handle the stressful situation in a healthy manner rather than prompt me to pop an antianxiety pill. But when you continuously feed your mind with unhealthy thoughts and scenarios—"OMG, I'm so stressed! This is horrible. I can't handle this. This is the worst day of my life. I want to die!"—your body becomes so overloaded by fight-or-flight hormones that it doesn't know how to react any differently, thus the trendy addiction to antianxiety medicines like Xanax.

"But," you may say, "Xanax is okay because my doctor prescribed it." Wrong! Xanax (just like similar medications) is still a substance you're dependent upon. We weren't made to be dependent upon any mood-altering substance, period! The power of suggestion is so true and life-changing! Feed your mind with healthy thoughts. No excuses. Do it! Your *choice*!

Notes

_____

_____

_____

_____

_____

_____

_____

_____

_____

_____

_____

_____

_____

_____

_____

_____

_____

_____

_____

_____

Notes

_____

_____

_____

_____

_____

_____

_____

_____

_____

_____

_____

_____

_____

_____

_____

_____

_____

_____

_____

_____

Chapter 7

Humility

Humility is key for health
Will bring us joy
Will bring us wealth

To be rich in money
Is not the key
To have self-worth
Means more to me

So humble yourself
So you can see
The better person
You're meant to be

List your shortcomings
One by one
Ask God to take them
till you're left with *none*

I'm not an addict
This too shall pass
I'm not an addict
I'm just an ass

Why is it so hard for human beings to humble themselves? The only thing I can come up with is that people think that asking for help is a sign of weakness. Some people think that weakness means you're stupid or a loser, and who wants to be either, right? So, it's better to pretend to be strong, smart, and a winner, even if it's killing you to do so. At least then your tombstone can read, "One smart, strong, winner *lies* here." Sounds pretty stupid to me!

It takes a real man to admit he was wrong. It takes a real woman to say, "I'm sorry." It takes a real person to accept an apology. And here's the thing: If you don't achieve humility, all your efforts to overcome your addition will be in vain. If you don't humble yourself, you won't fully achieve your goal of transforming your life. Fortunately, if you practice the art of humility long enough, it will eventually become an intrinsic part of who you are.

I grew up in a very strict Italian family. My brother and I not only got hit with a wooden spoon by our mom, but our aunts were welcome to whack us, too. We never heard "I love you," even though our relatives did love us. They simply could never humble themselves enough to say it. And forget about ever hearing "I'm sorry" from any of the adults!

Growing up being thought to be tough and smacked harder for crying was a very damaging thing for a child to experience, but guess what? I learned from television programs like *The Andy Griffith Show*, *The Partridge Family*, and *The Brady Bunch* that there was a better way to live. So, as tough as I was—and, believe me, I was one tough kid—I decided I needed to become humble and allow God to soften me up a bit.

I remember praying, "Okay, God. I don't want to be a tough bitch anymore, but please don't make me a wimp." I still want to be strong, but I also want to be gentle, accepting, caring, loving, and generous to a fault. (Yup, you read that right—to a fault.) But I will choose to maintain my rule that no abusers are allowed in my life. I've had people abuse me due to their drug, alcohol, food, gambling, and sexual addictions, and I always thought I could fix them. Nope! They're the only ones who can fix themselves. I now own—yup, own— the power to completely walk away. Humbling yourself doesn't mean you become a doormat. It means you can set healthy boundaries. I refuse to be an enabler!

Now, friends and family members of addicts, this section is for you. You always hear that you're supposed to stop enabling an addict. Well, enabling doesn't just mean feeding something; it also means tolerating and accepting it. Stop making excuses for the addict in your life. Stop allowing them to steal from you. Stop allowing them to abuse you mentally or physically. Know the role you play in the addict's life.

If you picked up this book so that you could help a loved one, then I'm here to guide you through that process. As I said in the beginning of this book, addiction isn't a disease, so stop treating it like it is. What you need to do is provide tough love, which has different levels and degrees. I don't believe in kicking an addict out of your life and ceasing all contact with them as long as they're willing to get the help they need. If you're being physically or mentally abused by this person, you need to save yourself first, before you can even start "saving" them.

The first step for helping an addict in your life is to accept what you're really dealing with. Don't sugarcoat it; it is what it is. Set your boundaries and stick to them. Your "yes" means yes and your "no" means no. Stop blaming the addict for all the suffering you're enduring in your life. You're contributing to the situation. Stop giving them money, a ride, and excuses. Stop pretending to believe their lies.

I went from being an addict and saving myself to thinking about how I could save another addict in my life. I tolerated the abuse, manipulation, and lies because I kept thinking that, because I was fixed, I could fix them. I fooled myself into believing that they'd be worse off without my help, but all I did was enable their behavior. I inadvertently allowed them to continue with their abuse because, once again, there was no way I could fix them. You can only fix yourself!

I've witnessed firsthand the fallout of being a true enabler—parents who gave their addict child money and housing, paid his bills, tolerated his behavior, accepted his lies, pretended he was fine, and conveyed a false image of a perfect life to outsiders, which ultimately caused his death. How tragic this was for me.

Know your role. Take a hard look at yourself. Is your enabling behavior your own addiction? Do you enable because, if you didn't have this person to "take care of," you might have to face your own demons and the issues in your own life? Do you think this person's addiction is a reflection on you? Will people judge you to be a bad parent because you raised a child who's an addict? Or is your significant other an addict because you aren't the best wife/husband/partner? Ask yourself these questions and self-evaluate. Someone else's addiction is *not* about you! You did nothing to lead this person into this behavior. But are you helping this person *stay* on the path of addiction?

You need to say no to an addict and stand by your word. Don't allow them to manipulate you. It's important not to judge this person. If they're reaching out for help, don't slap the hand that's reaching. Once the addict sees this and knows you're coming from a good, loving place, they'll trust that your intentions are good and unselfish. This person will now know that the support you give to them is part of a healthy and positive lifestyle, not one of destruction.

An addict may not always directly ask for help, and you may be waiting for them to hit rock bottom. There's no need to wait for that to happen, however. Have a conversation with this person. Sit down, just the two of you, and call them out on how their addiction is affecting you.

I'm not a big believer in group interventions. Who wants to be attacked by multiple people all at once? But sitting down with an addict, calling them out on all their crap, and letting them hear these things directly from your mouth may just open up the door to them telling you that they need help. They may know they need help and may have wanted it for a long time, but you, as an enabler, made it easy for them to continue their behavior since there were never any permanent consequences.

Remember when you were a child and you did

something bad? Maybe your parents took away your favorite toy, gave you a time-out, or sent you to your room. Well, you knew you'd eventually get that toy back and that you'd leave your room at some point. But what about the day when your loved one looked you in the eyes, really called you out on something, and told you how much you'd disappointed them. Hearing that word, *disappointed*, was worse than any punishment you could have received.

Today, as an enabler, *you* may be the person who's the disappointment, because what your loved one needs when they're spiraling closer and closer toward rock bottom isn't your tolerance of their situation—it's your honesty. Don't bring a shovel and help them dig their own grave. Instead, take away their shovel and knock them over the head with it, saying, "You are *not* going to die. You're going to live." Then, take their hand and guide them away from that grave. Show them that you're there for them in a positive way. Go with them to church or go with them to the grocery store and help them make healthy choices. Bring them to positive places. You have to change with them. Allow the positive behavior to fill both your lives; don't contribute to anything negative. Your *choice*!

Notes

_____

_____

_____

_____

_____

_____

_____

_____

_____

_____

_____

_____

_____

_____

_____

_____

_____

_____

_____

_____

Notes

_____

_____

_____

_____

_____

_____

_____

_____

_____

_____

_____

_____

_____

_____

_____

_____

_____

_____

Chapter 8

Willingness

The key to change
Is willingness
To stay the same
Is brokenness
Without this key
There's emptiness
Now take control
And clean your mess

Make amends to those
That you have harmed
Through selfishness
That you once charmed

You lied, you stole
You cheated them
You had them think
You were a gem

Now cut the crap
For once be real
Tell them the truth
On how you feel

I'm not an addict
this too shall pass
I'm not an addict
I'm just an ass

You may have screwed over so many people during the course of your addiction that righting your wrongs might seem impossible. If you think something is impossible, that leaves you feeling hopeless, and feeling hopeless is one of the worst feelings ever. To deal with this hopelessness, you have two options.

One option is to indulge in a pity party—"Woe is me. Life sucks. Everything always goes wrong no matter how hard I try"—which is simply an excuse to continue on your self-righteous path of destruction. The other option is to step up to the plate like a champ, look out into the field, assess your situation, and slowly start to swing at your first ball. Strike one. Okay, take a deep breath. Position yourself for ball two. Damn, strike two. Okay, one more shot. Ready? Breathe and then swing. Guess what? You hit the ball. You made it to first base.

You see where I'm going with this? You have to start somewhere. I promise that if you continue to move forward without going backwards, ultimately you'll end up on second base and then third. And, get this: it may take you a while, but, eventually, you'll definitely hit a home run.

Now, here's the bad news. No matter how hard you try, no matter how many wrongs you make right, there will always be someone who won't accept your apology and won't believe that you've changed. But now for the good news again: That doesn't matter! You and God know your heart. You know your intentions and you know your worth. I promise you that, as enough times passes, even those doubters will be thinking, "Hmm, maybe he or she *has* changed."

A willingness to change is the most important step in recovery. It's so worth it! Your *choice*.

Notes

_____

_____

_____

_____

_____

_____

_____

_____

_____

_____

_____

_____

_____

_____

_____

_____

_____

_____

Notes

_____

_____

_____

_____

_____

_____

_____

_____

_____

_____

_____

_____

_____

_____

_____

_____

_____

_____

_____

_____

Chapter 9

Forgiveness

Forgiveness starts
Within yourself
Put all your trash
Up on a shelf

Don't forget
What you have done
But clean it up
One by one

Ask God to forgive you
Once and for all
Get off your high horse
And learn how to crawl

To the people you hurt
You must make amends
Reach out to your family
And all your old friends

If you truly are sorry
And this they will know
Not by your words
But the actions you show

They may now forgive you
Or maybe they won't
As far as using and lying
I warn you, just don't

I'm not an addict
This too shall pass
I'm not an addict
I'm just an ass

Okay, guys, here comes the hard part: forgiving yourself. This can actually be a lot harder than asking other people for forgiveness. Many addicts have done some pretty bad things while using. Some of you reading this book right now are in jail, and you deserve to be there. When you're truly sorry for something, only you and God can know that for certain. Actions speak louder than words, so stop with the lip service. The people you've hurt hate that crap! Being all talk and no action only makes you more of a horrible person. Say what you mean and mean what you say. Then and only then can you forgive yourself. Until then, you will stay f'd up.

I'm going to share with you the best way to start making amends with the people you've hurt. First, block off a day that you can spend by yourself. Then, throughout that day, make a list of everyone you hurt in some way because of your addiction, and organize those people into categorizes of how important they are to you. Then, look at the people who are at the bottom of that list—say, acquaintances rather than close friends or family members—and write them a brief note, saying that you no longer use, have been doing some soul-searching, would like to apologize to them, and, if possible, rectify what you did. As you progress up your list to the more important people, your notes should turn into letters. When it comes to your closest friends and family members, you must pour out your heart and soul to them. Ask them for forgiveness and make promises you will no longer break. You can do this! Your *choice*!

Notes

_____

_____

_____

_____

_____

_____

_____

_____

_____

_____

_____

_____

_____

_____

_____

_____

_____

_____

_____

_____

_____

Notes

_____

_____

_____

_____

_____

_____

_____

_____

_____

_____

_____

_____

_____

_____

_____

_____

_____

_____

Chapter 10

Maintenance

You need to maintain
An honest, good life
No more backstabbing
Like a thief with a knife

Take personal notes
On how you are doing
Keep everything honest
So nothing is stewing

Perfect we're not
But keep this in mind
If you do something wrong
Make it right and be kind

I'm not an addict
This too shall pass
I'm not an addict
I'm just an ass

Here's the thing: So many addicts maintain their so-called sobriety by lying on a daily basis. They go to meetings every week and gloat over their sobriety, and some may even be sponsors to unsuspecting newcomers. Why? Glad you asked. Because they're pathological liars who can only feel good about themselves. You know who you are. If you truly want to live a healthy life, you need to *maintain* a sober life. Period.

Living a sober life involves so much more than just not picking up. It means living a life that's filled with loyalty, honesty, friendship, and a healthy family setting as well as not going from one addiction to another. Just because you're not using your so-called drug of choice doesn't mean you can substitute it with something else. If you do that, then you're still maintaining an addictive lifestyle. Do you get it? You can't stop using drugs and start drinking instead, you can't stop gambling in excess and start looking for sex from several partners, and you can't stop smoking cigarettes and start overeating until you're sick. Now do you get it? By the end of the book, you *will* get it! Then it will be *your choice* whether you change or not!

Notes

_____

_____

_____

_____

_____

_____

_____

_____

_____

_____

_____

_____

_____

_____

_____

_____

_____

_____

_____

_____

Notes

_____

_____

_____

_____

_____

_____

_____

_____

_____

_____

_____

_____

_____

_____

_____

_____

_____

_____

_____

Chapter 11

Making Contact

Make contact with God
Through prayer and his will
Continue to climb
Up over that hill

Keep seeking what's right
And you'll never fall
If you do all that's wrong
You'll continue to crawl

So seek out your God
And ask him to guide you
On how you should live
And ask him to find you

I'm not an addict
This too shall pass
I'm not an addict
I'm just an ass

Make contact with God and your inner self on a daily
basis. Keep a personal inventory every day and pray
to God to help you see your shortcomings and to help

you fix them. Seek out and reconnect with healthy people who share your faith. If necessary, go to church or to prayer meetings, and ask a sober, healthy friend or family member to allow you to connect with them daily. Do whatever it takes to stay sober within healthy parameters. Do it! No excuses! Your *choice*.

Remember how earlier I said that my earthly father was no different than my Heavenly Father? Well, think of God as *your* Heavenly Father. It's never too late to call on him. God never sleeps, and he's never involved with anything more important than you at any moment in time. God is at your disposal. Who could ask for more than that?

This doesn't mean that you must go to church every week, that you can never hang out with non-Christian friends, or that you have to be perfect. Those ideas are a joke, and if anyone tries to make you believe them just smile and walk away.

Calling upon God isn't a religion; it's a relationship between you and your dad! Yup, that's right. There's not a day that goes by that I don't talk to him. I'm either thanking him, asking for his help, or, heck, even arguing with him. "No way, God. I'm not doing that!" Guess what? By the end of the argument—you guessed it—I am *so* doing that. Ugh, I hate when that happens! It may not be right away, but I swear to you, I always end up seeing the benefit of my submission to God. I usually giggle and say, "Uh-huh, of course!"

Notes

_____

_____

_____

_____

_____

_____

_____

_____

_____

_____

_____

_____

_____

_____

_____

_____

_____

_____

_____

_____

Notes

_____

_____

_____

_____

_____

_____

_____

_____

_____

_____

_____

_____

_____

_____

_____

_____

_____

_____

_____

Chapter 12

Service

Service to others
It sure seems far-fetched
From a selfish addict
Whose truths were stretched

Through your addiction
You did no good
Your motives all sucked
Now change if you would

You can be the bad guy
Or you can be good
You can act out in rage
Or calm like you should

The choice is yours
So look and see
Which one of these
Are you *choosing* to be?

I'm not an addict
This too shall pass
I'm not an addict
I'm just an ass

Addicts are the most selfish and lazy "F'N" people in the world. Yes, you are! That makes you a horrible person. Animals are much more caring than you. If you don't want to be that kind of person, then *change*! Yup, it's that simple. It's up to you. I know it's hard, but start slowly. Begin by waking up early every day. Make your damn messy bed. Eat something healthy. Go to a shelter and donate one hour of your time. Start there. Trust me, if you ever want to feel important or good about yourself, that will do it.

People will never believe that you've truly changed if you simply *say* you have. Actions speak louder than words. Start changing yourself by helping someone else, and then continue to do so. Get a job if you don't already have one. It doesn't matter what you do as long as you do something.

If you continue to only serve your own selfish needs, you will never heal. You must break that horrible, disgusting habit once and for all. Put others' needs first, and start being that person you were created to be! Seek God daily to help you with your selfishness, and, I promise, he will transform you in that area. Your *choice*!

Notes

_____

_____

_____

_____

_____

_____

_____

_____

_____

_____

_____

_____

_____

_____

_____

_____

_____

_____

Notes

_____

_____

_____

_____

_____

_____

_____

_____

_____

_____

_____

_____

_____

_____

_____

_____

_____

_____

Chapter 13

Put Down The Gun

I had to have
This purple gun
Just in case
My life was done

I kept it safe
Locked in my room
'Cause I was filled
With gloom and doom

Yes, there were times
That I just knew
If I loaded it up
What I could do

But I kept on hearing
That gentle voice
Put down that gun
You have that *choice*

Life may seem hard
At the end of the day
That's when you need
To really pray

"Dear Father, I beg you
To show me the truth.
How can life be so bad
When I'm only a youth?"

Get rid of that gun
And go take a shower
Ask someone for help
You do have that power!

I can almost guarantee you that every person at some point in their lives has felt hopeless, depressed, sad, or anxious. If they hadn't, they wouldn't be human. You are not alone. We hear every day that someone famous has lost his or her life to drugs, alcohol, depression, or suicide. We can't fathom that someone so famous, so rich, and so loved felt hopeless, worthless, or desperate. People are people. Sometimes we're our own worst enemy. Make a decision to be your best friend. Love yourself, love your neighbor. Make conscious efforts to move forward in a healthy manner.

When I say, "Put down that gun," that can mean to literally put down the damn gun, your life is worth living, or it can be referring, metaphorically, to another "gun," something that is *slowly* killing you: your addiction. There's always someone out there that you can contact. There are shelters, safe houses, hospitals, and many other options. Someone, someplace, is always available to help you. Please choose to be healthy. Please choose to never use again. Please choose to pray to God for help. Please choose life, not death.

Remember, it's always, *your choice*!

Notes

_____

_____

_____

_____

_____

_____

_____

_____

_____

_____

_____

_____

_____

_____

_____

_____

_____

_____

Notes

_____

_____

_____

_____

_____

_____

_____

_____

_____

_____

_____

_____

_____

_____

_____

_____

_____

_____

_____

_____

_____

Chapter 14

Change: Your Choice

I had a life-changing moment
That I knew had to be
The only way to change things
Was to first start with me

So I looked in the mirror
And woke up one day
And thought to myself
I needed to pray

So I asked God to change me
To help me stay strong
To clean up my mess
To right what's been wrong

I cleaned up my diet
I cleaned up my room
I cleaned up old habits
With this old dirty broom

I kept going forward
And never looked back
I refused to derail
Stayed on the right track

I realize my worth
and all that did matter
Through my selfish behavior
The lives that I shattered

I finally decided
At thirty years old
To stop abusing my body
My mind, heart, and soul

My life-changing choice
That I had once made
Over twenty-five years now
My debt has been paid

So you read all my thoughts
On how to stay clean
It's all or nothing, my friend
There's no in-between

To live or to die
Is a choice you must make
Your life is not worthless
You're not a mistake

One day at a time
Is a slogan you've heard
It works if you work it
While applying his word

For you to get healthy
For your mind not to fail
Escaping reality
Will keep you in jail

With addictive behavior
Sex, drugs, food, or money
Substituting addictions?
Now isn't that funny!

I'm not an addict
This too shall pass
I'm not an addict
I'm just an ass!

May the good lord bless you and guide you!

From this page forward is my revised addition

"2020"

All of my accomplishments since I changed my life 29 years ago.

- 1993 Became a Certified Fasting & Detox Coach
- 2001 I won two poetry contest where they published my poems
- 2008 Became a Vegan Chef from The Natural Gourmet Institute
- 2016 Became a Nutritional Health Coach
- April 2016 Became a Published Author
- From September 2016 to recent Became an Internet Radio Show Host and proud to be part of Hamilton Radio, PA NJ Radio, Beverly Nation Network, D.A.M.O.N Looks Network, & Remember Then Radio.
- March 2019 I received a Certificate of Merit for broadcasting out of Germany with a Nomination for 2019 Internet International Hall of Fame
- December 2019 I was incredibly honored to be Inducted into the Hall of Fame for broadcasting
- January 2019 Became a recovery coach.

The reason I listed all my accomplishments is to show you, it's never too late no matter how old you are, to change your life. If anyone would have ever told me at thirty years old when I stopped using drugs that any of this was possible, I would have laughed in their face.

Who would have thought that 29 years later I would be walking back into Princeton House Rehab Center for the first time since I left there 30 years ago, holding my books on Addiction. God is so Faithful.

During this process of adding to this this book I found my old journal from Princeton House. It took me a whole week to go through all my notes which brought about old memories and anxiety. Reading letters I wrote to myself brought me to tears. The first time in a long time, I allowed myself to experience the feeling I once felt. A big part of me could not believe what I was reading "Was that really me" I wish my older self could have spoken to my younger self. In retrospect, my older self is now speaking to you, thanks to my younger self. My hope here is that you can take what I'm saying to heart and save your life. Thank God for my experiences, because I'm here today being able to save lives. Since my book was published and I really put myself out there, one might say I'm an open book.

Being an open book has not only helped myself tremendously after the last four years, it's also helped saved lives of so many friends and family members who realized they can now come to me. I'm going to tell you all a story that will really freak you out. About a year after my book was published and posted all over Facebook, a strange man reached out to me asking about my book. This man was not only in a sober living home he was almost two years clean and sober, after facetiming with him, I recognized his eyes. Low and behold, he used to be my dealer. Imagine that, my ex drug dealer reaching out to me on my book on addiction. Not only did my book help save his life, one might say I'm now his recovery coach. This man who was an Atheist, came to know Christ through me. Another Affirmation, thank you God!

"Face it...'till U Make It"

FAKE IT 'TIL U MAKE IT
IS A TERM HEARD SO MUCH
I DON'T REALLY AGREE
IT'S LIVING WITH A CRUTCH

NOT JUST FOR ADDICTION
ALL LIFE LESSONS MY FRIEND
THAT'S A SADDENED LIFE
TO LIVE UNTIL THE END

I'D RATHER GO BY
A SAYING MORE REAL
"FACE IT 'TILL U MAKE IT"
IN SPITE OF HOW U FEEL!

WE GOTTA GROW UP
PUT OUR PASTS BEHIND
IN SPITE OF OUR HURTS
THERE'S GREATNESS TO FIND

I'D RATHER GO THROUGH LIFE
SMILING EVERYDAY
HOLDING UP MY CHIN
ALL GOOD THINGS TO SAY

POSITIVE THINKING
& ACTIONS LIKEWISE
THROW OUT A FORCE
UP INTO THE SKIES

WHAT WE PROJECT
IS WHAT WE WILL EARN
KARMA IS REAL
WE EACH HAVE A TURN

YOUR THOUGHTS R WIRED
TO MAKE YOU THINK
WHIT WHAT YOU DO
CAN MAKE YOU SINK

KEEP ALL YOUR THOUGHTS
UPLIFTING & REAL
FEEDING YOUR MIND CRAP
DESTROYS HOW YOU FEEL

SO DON'T PUT OUT CRAP
IT COMES BACK TO BITE
STAND UP REAL TALL
& JUST FIGHT THE FIGHT

I PROMISE YOU THIS
IF YOU FACE ALL YOUR FEARS
IT MAY BE QUITE SCARY
BUT WILL ADD TO YOUR YEARS

ONE DAY YOU'LL BE HAPPY
WITH WHO YOU NOW ARE
JUST LOOK AT ME
I'VE REALLY COME FAR

I LOOK IN THE MIRROR
& LIKE WHAT I SEE
BUT MOST IMPORTANT
I REALLY LOVE ME!

GERI

Notes

_____

_____

_____

_____

_____

_____

_____

_____

_____

_____

_____

_____

_____

_____

_____

_____

_____

_____

Notes

_____

_____

_____

_____

_____

_____

_____

_____

_____

_____

_____

_____

_____

_____

_____

_____

_____

_____

_____

_____

Divine

Chapter 15

Divine Intervention

This chapter is going to reference some of what I wrote in chapter five about being touched by an older man. Since I was a young teenager and he was in his late twenties, I always felt like I let a Child molester go. I wrote about doing drugs because I couldn't live with that. My relationship with God has grown incredibly strong over the last thirty years. Once again God has come through and lifted that great weight off my shoulders I've been carrying since I was a teenager. A few years ago, for the first time since the incident I was reacquainted with this man at an outing. I'm in my late 50's he's in his late 70's and he snuck up behind me and grabbed my butt. (I know what your all thinking, I should of punched him in his face) Instead I smiled, looked up at God and was grateful he gave me an affirmation and showed me that this man was a perverted old man and not a child molester. If he was a child molester, he would not have been interested in me in my fifties Once again God came through for me, that burden has now been lifted, once and for all.

"Abuse"

WHILE WRITING THIS POEM
MY HEART SURE WILL BREAK
ABUSE TOWARDS A CHILD
CAUSES A CHILD TO ACHE

NOT JUS FOR A MOMENT
OR EVEN A YEAR
A LIFETIME OF SORROW
AS IN...4EVER, I FEAR.

A CHILD IS HELPLESS
SHOULD BE CARED FOR & FED
NOT ABUSED & DISRESPECTED
TORTURED & LEFT FOR DEAD.

THE MONSTERS THAT DO THIS
DEATH SENTENCE SHOULD AWAIT
THAT POOR CHILD WAS STRIPPED
NOW IN OUR HANDS IS HIS FATE

THE MONSTERS THAT DO THIS
SHOULD B PUT TO DEATH...
FOR THE CHILD THEY DESTROYED
LET THEM TAKE THEIR LAST BREATH!

THEY SHOULD NOT SERVE IN JAIL
WTF...THEY SERVE THEIR TIME?!
4EVER A CHILD IS DAMAGED
BUT THEY GET AWAY WITH THIS CRIME?!

THEY ARE NOT HUMAN
NOT HEALTHY OR SANE
THEY'RE SUFFERING TOO
PUT THEM OUT OF THEIR PAIN!

WE NEED TO BE MORE STRICT
WHEN IT COMES TO BREAKING LAWS
WHEN PEOPLE RAPE & MURDER
THE PUNISHMENT SHOULD FIT THE CAUSE!

CHILD ABUSE IS ALSO TOWARDS BOYS
NOT JUST FEMALES ALONE
STEP UP TO THE PLATE PEOPLE
ABUSE NEEDS TO BE KNOWN!

HOW ADULTS JUST IGNORE
I CAN NEVER CONCEIVE
THEY TOO ARE SICK
THIS TRUTH PLEASE BELIEVE!

IT'S SO MUCH DEEPER
THAN WE'LL EVER KNOW
CRIME AGAINST KIDS
IS THE LOWEST OF LOW!

DOMESTIC VIOLENCE
IS SECOND IN LINE
AT LEAST THEY'RE ADULTS
ACCEPTING THIS CRIME!

MOST IS TOWARDS WOMAN
& THEIR R SUM MEN
REGARDLESS OF SEX
IT HAPPENS TIME & AGAIN!

IF U ARE INVOLVED
IN BEING ABUSED
IT'S TIME U ARE HEARD
STOP BEING CONFUSED!

THERE IS SO MUCH HELP
IF U WANT IT TO END
U DO HAVE A VOICE
PLEASE SPEAK TO A FRIEND!

THERE IS HELP OUT THERE
ASK NOW PLEASE DON'T WAIT
REACH OUT TO THEM NOW
BEFORE IT'S TOO LATE!

STOP BEING A VICTIM
STAND UP 4 YOURSELF
PLEASE FACE YOUR FEARS
STORE THEM HIGH ON A SHELF

SEEK OUT THE LORD
HE'S NOT FAR AWAY
IF YOU ASK HIM FOR HELP
HE CAN SAVE YOU TODAY!

GERI 😞

Notes

_____

_____

_____

_____

_____

_____

_____

_____

_____

_____

_____

_____

_____

_____

_____

_____

_____

_____

_____

_____

Notes

_____

_____

_____

_____

_____

_____

_____

_____

_____

_____

_____

_____

_____

_____

_____

_____

_____

_____

_____

Chapter 16

My Story

Cool story, bro. STAY TUNED!!!!!!!!!!!!!!!!!!!!!!!!!!!!!!!!

My Story !!

I THOUGHT I'D SHARE MY STORY
IN A MORE POETIC WAY
TO GIVE U GUYS SUM INSITE
ON WHAT I WANNA SAY

I GREW UP IN A CRAZY ITALIAN HOME
WHERE BOUNDARIES DID NOT EXIST
NO SUCH THING AS PERSONAL SPACE
AS I GREW UP I STARTED TO RESIST

MY SIGN IS A PISCES
& IT REALLY HOLDS TRUE
I'M ARTISTIC & CURIOUS
WITH ALL THAT I DO

MY HEART ON MY SLEEVE
IS WHERE IT WAS WORN
THAT GOOD & THAT BAD FISH
ALWAYS MADE ME FEEL TORN

EVERYTHING POSSIBLE
THERE WAS TO EXPLORE
MY BUCKET LIST WAS HUGE
EVERYDAY I WANTED MORE

IT GOT ME INTO TROUBLE
FROM ART SCHOOL INTO DRUGS
TRAVELING ALL OVER THE WORLD
EVEN TASTING SUM BUGS

GETTING PREGNANT THAN MARRIED
& OFCOURSE CAME DIVORCE
I LIVED MY SELF UNMANAGEABLE
CHALLENGED EVERYTHING WITH FORCE

OUTSIDE OF THE BOX
IS WHERE I BELONGED
BUT I ALWAYS MADE RIGHT
WHATEVER I WRONGED

I FOUGHT STRUCTURE & RULES
& NEVER REGRETTED
I ONLY WORRIED WHEN NEEDED
SMALL STUFF...NEVER SWEATED

BEING SELF EMPLOYED TOO YOUNG
& MAKING TOO MUCH MONEY
IT GOT ME INTO TROUBLE
NOW LIFE... WAS NOT SO FUNNY

BEING SO YOUNG
& BEING SO SICK
I WOKE UP & THOUGHT
I NEED HELP QUICK!

SO I STOPPED ALL THE CRAP
& BEGGED GOD TO HEAR ME
HE SAVED ME THAT DAY
& HE DECIDED TO SPARE ME

HE SAVED MY LIFE
& GAVE ME MY CALLING
NOW GO HELP OTHERS
THE ONES THAT ARE FALLING

MY ENTIRE LIFE
SINCE I WAS YOUNG
WAS FINDING THE BROKEN
WHO I WAS AMONG

25 YRS. LATER
GOD SAID...WRITE OUR BOOK
I SMILED & THOUGHT OK
NOW I KNOW ...THIS IS WHAT IT TOOK

I'LL NEVER REGRET MY CHOICES
CAUSE I'M THE PERSON I AM TODAY
I'LL ALWAYS PAY IT FORWARD
IF I CAN HELP IN ANY WAY

HEALTH COACHING'S MY PASSION
ON MY RADIO SHOW TOO
I LUV HELPING OTHERS
IT'S WHAT I'M MADE TO DO!

MY LIFE CHANGING CHOICE
THAT I HAD ONCE MADE
OVER 26 YRS. NOW
MY DEBT HAS BEEN PAID

GERI

"Integrity"

DO U EVEN KNOW
HOW TO B TRUE
TO YOURSELF & OTHERS
I'M ASKING U!

IF U LOOK IN THE MIRROR
DO U LIKE WHAT U SEE
OR DO U SHY AWAY
OR R U LIKE ME?

I DON'T TRY TO BE
SOMEONE I'M NOT
I DO NOT PRETEND
TO HAVE MORE THAN I GOT!

U SEE TO ME
WHAT DOES MATTER MOST
R PEOPLE IN GENERAL
SO PLEASE DON'T U BOAST...

ON HOW GREAT U R...
WITH ALL OF YOUR LOOT
& THE THINGS THAT U HAVE
WITH THAT HORN THAT U TOOT...

CAUSE IF U DON'T SHARE
WITH PEOPLE IN NEED,
U BECOME YOUR OWN KING
FILLED WITH ANGER & GREED!

I DO LUV THE LORD
HE MADE ME THIS WAY
HE TAUGHT ME MY WORTH
& HOW TO LIVE EACH DAY...

DO U HAVE INTEGRITY
DO U REALLY NOT CARE
WHO'S FEET U STEP OVER
LIFE JUST SEEMS UNFAIR...

WHAT WILL IT TAKE
TO GET BACK WHAT WE HAD
CAUSE THE WAY WERE TREATING PEOPLE
IS DISGUSTING & SAD...

IT DOESN'T SEEM TO ME
THAT PEOPLE WANNA CHANGE
THEY'D RATHER GO THROUGH LIFE
LIKE ON A FIREING RANGE!

CAUSE IN THE END
WHICH WE ALL WILL SEE
AS WE TAKE OUR LAST BREATH
WHO DO U WANNA BE...

THAT HORRIBLE GUY
THE LIAR, THE THIEF...
OR THE GUY THEY ALL TRUSTED,
THEYRE LEFT WITH THIS GRIEF!

SO MAKE A CHOICE
ON WHO TO BE
I HOPE U CHOOSE WISELY
ON WHO U SHOULD BE!

GERI ☺

"Balance"

LIFE IS MADE OF CHOICES
WE ALL MUST PICK & CHOOSE
WE NEED TO BE REAL CAREFUL
WHEN BREAKING ALL THE RULES

IM NOT SAYING BE BORING
OR NEVER TO HAVE FUN
BUT TRY TO KEEP A BALANCE
WITH THINGS THAT U HAVE DONE

SOMETIMES TOO MUCH OF ANYTHING
MAY HURT U IN THE END
TOO MUCH FOOD...OR SEX...OR CASH
COULD COST U A GOOD FRIEND

SO MAINTAIN A BALANCE
IN ALL U DO
YOUR SANITY
IS UP TO U

FOR U TO B HEALTHY
ITS NOT JUS YOUR FOOD
YOUR THOUGHTS SHOULD BE STABLE
TO CONTROL YOUR GOOD MOOD

YOUR HOME SHOULD BE CLEAN
SO U DON'T GET SICK
FROM HARMFUL BACTERIA
THAT SUCKS LIKE A TICK

EVEN THE PEOPLE
WITH TIME U DO SPEND
CHOOSE YOUR FRIEDS WISELY
OR U WILL LOSE IN THE END

MY CHOICES I MAKE
FROM WHEN I WAS YOUNG
HAVE SURELY CHANGED NOW
MY THOUGHTS HAVE NOW SWUNG

IF YOUR LOOKING TO FIND
WHAT THE KEY TO LIFE SHOULD BE
ITS ALL UP TO U FRIEND
CAUSE U OWN THE KEY

GERI 😊

"Utilizing Gifts & Talents"

WE ARE BORN WITH TALENTS
WE ARE BORN WITH DRIVE
WITH DIFFERENT GIFTS
TO HELP US THRIVE

I KNEW EARLY ON
I WAS BORN TO DRAW & PAINT
TO ALSO WRITE POETRY
& TO TALK WITHOUT RESTRAINT

OUR GIFTS & TALENTS
SHOULD ALL BE USED
GOD'S GIFT TO US
NOT BE ABUSED

WE CAN GO FAR
IN LIFE FOR SURE
USING OUR GIFTS
TO GO ON TOUR

ALL OUR TALENTS SHOULD B USED
TO CREATE OURSELVES & MORE
THEN OUR JOB'S TO SHARE THEM
TO EVEN UP THE SCORE

YOU SEE IN LIFE WHAT'S NEEDED
IS NOT JUST FOR OURSELVES
ONCE OUR GIFTS ARE MASTERED
TAKE THEM OFF THE SHELVES

A LIVING WE CAN MAKE
BY SPREADING THEM AROUND
NOT JUST FOR THE MONEY
TO SPREAD A PEACEFUL SOUND

DON'T TAKE FOR GRANTED
THE GIFTS YOUR GIVEN
GO OUT & SPREAD THE JOY...
OUR GIFTS ARE NOT
TO BE HELD BACK
FOR US TO SELF DESTROY...

PUT YOUR EFFORTS FORTH
DO NOT HESITATE
ALL YOUR TALENTS MY FRIEND
ARE NEVER SECOND RATE

NEVER HOLD THEM BACK
OR YOU WILL SURELY DIE
MAYBE NOT IN BODY
BUT YOUR SOUL WILL CRY

OUR GIFTS WERE MADE TO SHARE
OUR TALENTS MADE TO SOAR
GO THROUGH LIFE ENLIGHTENED
& THEN YOU CAN ROAR!

BE PROUD OF WHO YOU ARE
BE HAPPY YOU'RE ALIVE
ONCE AGAIN MY FRIEND
YOUR GIFTS WILL HELP U THRIVE!

BY PUTTING EFFORTS FORTH
NOT KEEPING THEM AT BAY
YOUR NAME WILL LIVE FOREVER
FOREVER & A DAY!

GO THROUGH LIFE EXCITED
FOR WHAT YOU SURE CAN GIVE
TO YOURSELF & OTHERS
IS OUR REASON TO LIVE

OUR GRAVE WILL BE QUITE LONELY
BUT OUR LEGACY LIVES ON
MAKE SURE PEOPLE SMILE
WITH THE BREAKING DAWN

GERI

"Artist"

I LUV TO DRAW
N JUS CREATE
PAINT WITH A BRUSH
I JUS CAN'T WAIT

TO B CREATIVE
IS WHAT I DO
TAKE SOMETHING OLD
N MAKE IT NEW

I LUV USING CHARCOAL
& I LUV USING INK
WHEN I FEEL CREATIVE
MY MIND STARTS TO THINK

NOW WHAT COULD I DO
TO MAKE THIS LOOK GOOD
MY MIND NEVER STOPS
IF ONLY IT COULD

I'M AN ARTIST & POET
A WRITER & CHEF
I LUV TO CREATE
MY BRAIN DON'T GO LEFT

GOD MADE ME RIGHT BRAINED
SO I COULD HAVE FUN
OR I WOULD GO CRAZY
FAR AWAY I WOULD RUN

MY ART KEEPS ME GROUNDED
AS SANE AS COULD BE
CAUSE WITH NO PINK CRAYONS
NO RAINBOWS FOR ME

I HAVE TO PUT COLOR
IN ALL THAT I DO
BECAUSE OF THE COLORS
I NEVER FEEL BLUE!

GERI

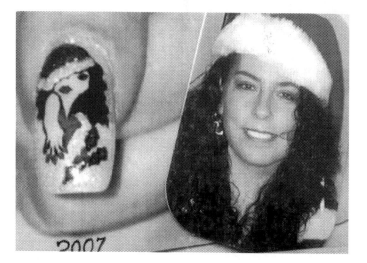

Chef Geri !

WHO LUVS TO EAT
ALL KINDS OF FOOD
IF U R ITALIAN
NOT EATING...IS RUDE!

AN ITALIAN KID
GROWS UP FAT
FOOD IS THE ANSWER
FOR THIS OR FOR THAT

SO WE LEARN HOW TO COOK
WHEN WERE ONLY A KID
TO BRIBE ALL OUR FRIENDS
THIS IS SOMETHING I DID!

I GOT WHAT I WANTED
& THEY ALL GOT FED
ESPECIALLY MOMS CUPCAKES
I TRADED FOR "BREAD"!

AS IN BREAD
I MEAN DOUGH
AS IN MONEY
U KNOW!

SO I CAUGHT ON QUICK
ON HOW TO KEEP FRIENDS
IF DA FOOD EVER STOPPED
OUR FRIENDSHIPS WOULD END!

FOOD CAN CURE ALL YOUR AILMENTS
FROM SADNESS TO JOY
CAN CURE A DISEASE
ORGANIC & SOY!

A VEGAN CHEF
IS WHAT I BECAME
TO HELP HEAL YOUR SICKNESS
IN GODS HOLY NAME!

MY FOOD IS AMAZING
U JUS NEED A TASTE
AFTER UR FIRST BITE
NOT A CRUMB WILL U WASTE!

MY FOOD N MY LUV
DO NOT SHOW DISFAVOR
FROM HOMELESS TO STARS
ILL FEED ALL WITHOUT WAVER!

JESUS HIMSELF,
5,000 HE FED
SO ILL KEEP ON FEEDING,
CAUSE THATS WHAT HE SAID!

GOD BLESSED ME WITH TALENTS
FROM SO LONG AGO
IF I LET THEM B WASTED
A BAD EXAMPLE I'D SHOW

SO TO ALL THE CHEFS
I WANNA SAY
KEEP FEEDING PEOPLE
EACH & EVERY DAY!

GERI 😊

"Choose Wisely"

A healthy out look
Begins with you
A life fulfilled
Is up to you too

A healthy diet
Is where you start
But a healthy mind
Is the major part

Remove from your diet
All sugar my friend
all processed foods
kill in the end

Try being vegan
Or at least mostly greens
veggies will heal
even unhealthy genes

To get rid of toxins
Niacin's the key
Will remove even cravings
flushing out needs to be

Sugar is a drug
Your brain thinks it is
To get you real clean
Go take my quiz

The real way to detox
is not with a drug
It's through nutrition
and also a hug

Your brain sure can heal
I promise you this
If you do a cleanse
the drug you won't miss

Nutrition's the key
Do not be fooled
What NA is teaching
Must be over ruled!

You're in charge
Of life choices you make
Keeping them healthy
Is your journey to take

Life is made of choices
We all must pick and choose
We need to be real careful
When breaking all the rules

I'm not saying be boring
Or never have fun
But try to keep balance
With things you have done

Too much of anything
May hurt you in the end
Try to maintain balance
So not to lose a friend

Even the people
With time you do spend
Choose your friends wisely
Or you may lose in the end

The choices I made
From when I was young
Have surely changed
My thoughts have now swung

So "Know Your Worth"
say... "It Starts With Me"
You are the treasure
And You own the key!

GERI 😌

CHOOSE WISELY

Notes

_____

_____

_____

_____

_____

_____

_____

_____

_____

_____

_____

_____

_____

_____

_____

_____

_____

_____

Notes

_____

_____

_____

_____

_____

_____

_____

_____

_____

_____

_____

_____

_____

_____

_____

_____

_____

_____

_____

_____

_____

Chapter 17

"Niacin"

When I first wrote this book, I was unaware of Bill W's take on Niacin. What I'm going to share next is public knowledge and may shock you.

"A Public Blog"

When I gear up to read a blog I invariably have the same thought: Tell me something I don't know.

In this blog I am going to fulfill that promise for my readers since I have never encountered a psychotherapist or addiction counselor who knows what I am about to share. (If you are the one in a million exception, please accept my apology.) So make yourself comfortable and let's get this party started.

Let's begin with something you do know. In the summer of 1935 Bill W (aka Bill Wilson) and Dr. Bob (actually Dr. Bob Smith, birth name Robert Holbrook) conducted the first Alcoholics Anonymous or AA group. Since this initial meeting AA has helped more individuals than any group on record.

Make no mistake about it. Bill Wilson loved AA and he believed in it with every fiber in his body. But two key factors prohibited this from being the end of the story. First, although AA helped Bill W deal with his alcoholism, it did nothing to curb his anxiety and depression. Second, as powerful as AA was it didn't work for everybody.

Now fast forward from 1935 to the year 1960. Bill Wilson decided to attend a parapsychology conference in New York City. It was there that the famed British Writer and AA supporter, Aldous Huxley, introduced Wilson to two esteemed psychiatrists, Abram Hoffer and Humphrey Osmond.

These psychiatrists shared with Wilson a promising new treatment for alcoholics and schizophrenics dubbed vitamin B3 or niacin therapy. He was fascinated by their research.

Wilson began ingesting a bomber's load of the nutrient, 3 grams daily, only to report that his lifelong battle with depression and anxiety lifted in just 14 days! Is that amazing or what? I mean, seriously, it sounds like something right out of an infomercial airing at 2 AM after the one for Tony Robbins' self-improvement materials. Here was an ordinary over-the -counter vitamin that when ingested in the proper dosage was a fast acting remedy for alcoholism, depression, anxiety, and schizophrenia. And, as a side effect it helped lower the so-called bad cholesterol.

Wilson took immediate action and prescribed his miracle like intervention to AA friends who were described as educated. Others were said to be celebrities. According to Wilson, the results were nothing short of amazing.

Wilson was brimming with enthusiasm and forged on to share his knowledge with the doctors of AA. These were physicians who were alcoholics and therefore attending AA groups. But here is where the gauntlet began to fall and nothing was ever quite powerful enough to reverse the pattern.

The International Organization of AA, despite the fact that the members were appointed by Bill W, and he considered them friends, were not happy campers. Wilson, as they pointed out, was not a licensed physician and thus had no business extolling the virtues of vitamin therapy.

Bill Wilson spent the last eleven years of his life spreading the word about vitamin B3 therapy as a treatment option or supplement to AA groups. Wilson tried to rally the troops by creating three powerful booklets over the years to AA physicians, but it fell on deaf ears.

So who killed vitamin B3 or niacin therapy? Why was AA embraced by millions, while B3 niacin therapy never made it out of the starting blocks?

Certainly, I don't pretend to have *the* answer. Scores of reasons could be cited, but here are a few that just seem to make sense. Also keep in mind that nearly everybody is a great Monday morning quarterback. Had

I been in Bill W's shoes at the time I might have done exactly what he did.

Who killed vitamin B 3 niacin therapy?

1. The niacin flush. Unlike the tiny amount of B3 included in a typical multiple vitamin supplement, in order to import a clinical impact, the dose of niacin (also known as nicotinic acid) generally has to be high enough to induce a flush replete with itching and profound warmth. The effect is so pronounced that individuals taking niacin often mistake these symptoms for a heart attack or stroke and end up in the ER or an acute care facility. In all fairness, a very small percentage of the population finds the experience pleasurable.

2. AA traditions. Tradition six suggests AA won't endorse, finance, or lend the AA name to any outside enterprise or facility. Tradition ten suggests that AA has no opinions on outside issues, hence AA cannot become involved in a public controversy.

3. The American Psychiatric Association. In 1973 the organization revealed they could not duplicate Dr. Hoffer's data and therefore could not promote niacin therapy. Rumors surfaced that large doses of niacin caused liver problems. Hoffer, who boasted he took more B3 than anybody on the planet, remained healthy until he passed away at age 91. He denied all claims that niacin was responsible for liver difficulties and went as far as to say it promoted longevity.

Before he passed away he discovered a Canadian woman named Mary MacIsaac who took massive doses of B3 for 42 years. She practiced cross country skiing at age 110 and lived until age 112! Okay, I think I'll have what she was taking. Yes, it's clearly N=1 data, but I think it's safe to say that most supercentenarians don't spend the better part of the day on a ski slope.

4. Morbid fears related to the practice of orthomolecular psychiatry. Orthomolecular psychiatry (I'll pause while you Google it), a term coined by two time Nobel Prize recipient, Dr. Linus Pauling in 1968, is basically individualized mega-vitamin/nutrient therapy. B3 or niacin therapy fit neatly into this treatment category. The idea that patients might be diagnosing themselves and then heading for the nearest pharmacy or health food store to buy niacin on a BOGO sale just didn't sit well with mainstream psychiatrists. To be sure, the pharmaceutical companies marketing psychiatric medicinal were not overly thrilled either.

5. Forget the doctors of AA, Bill Wilson should have taken his message to the masses. I am thoroughly convinced that Bill W pitched his ideas to the wrong population. In my humble opinion if he had penned a self-help book on the topic B3 niacin therapy might well have become a household word. This was the 1960s and early 1970s for gosh sakes and titles like *I'm O.K.—You're O.K.*, *How to be Your Own Best Friend*,

and *Born to Win* were shaping American culture, not to mention the landscape of mental health.

Today, vestiges of niacin treatment live on in the minds of longevity seekers, the alternative health movement, and nutritionally minded cardiologists hell bent on shaving another silly little point off your LDL cholesterol score using straight niacin or a modern slow release version which may or may not eliminate flushing.

Had Bill W been successful in his mission to incorporate vitamin B3 niacin therapy into AA the entire face of addiction and mental health treatment might have looked very different today.

The story goes that before Bill Wilson passed away he was asked what he would like to be remembered for in the history books. Much to the chagrin of experts and those who have benefited from 12-step groups he chose niacin therapy over AA.

Who knew?

Notes

_____

_____

_____

_____

_____

_____

_____

_____

_____

_____

_____

_____

_____

_____

_____

_____

_____

_____

_____

Notes

Chapter 18

"Saved By Grace"

In spite of myself and the bad choices I've made, God never left me. I stayed faithful, in his promise to never leave me. I'm still a sinner, but through the blood of Jesus I'm now forgiven. I say that to say this, "Jesus is there for you too, put your faith in him before it's too late, and he can bring you out of any hardship you may be facing."

Geri Petito

"Christianity"

SO MANY RELIGIONS
HAVE SURFACED TODAY
MOST OF US WONDER
WHICH ONE'S THE RITE WAY

BEING BROUGHT UP CATHOLIC
I WASN'T A FAN
I ALWAYS STRUGGLED
WITH LISTENING TO MAN

I JUS WASN'T BUYING
THE CRAP THAT THEY SAID
MY SALVATION'S IN JESUS
THROUGH HIS BLOOD, HE SHED

NOT SACRAMENTS,
& GIVING CASH
CONFESSIONAL BOOTHS
& WEDNESDAYS ASH

THESE RULES THEY SPEAK OF
ARE ALL MAN MADE
IF YOU OPEN THE BIBLE
MANS WORDS WILL FADE

U WON'T FIND THEM IN THERE
'CAUSE GOD SAID IT CLEAR
U WON'T WORK YOUR WAY
INTO HEAVEN MY DEAR

MOST BIG RELIGIONS
HAVE PUT GOD AWAY
THEY WANT YOUR ALLIANCE
& WHAT YOU CAN PAY

WITH JESUS NAILED UPON THAT CROSS
BEFORE HIS LAST BREATH HE TOOK
HIS WORDS WERE SPOKEN FOR US TO HEAR
IT IS FINISHED...& LEFT US HIS BOOK

I TELL U THE TRUTH
THERE'S ONLY ONE GOD
WHEN U TAKE YOUR LAST BREATH
HE'LL GREET YOU & NOD

I HOPE YOU ARE READY
TO MEET HIM THAT DAY
WANNA HEAR HIM SAY WELL DONE
INSTEAD OF CASTING U AWAY

MY WORKS R JUST WORTHLESS
I'D END UP IN HELL
THAT'S WHY HE SENT JESUS
NOW IN HEAVEN, I'LL DWELL!

GERI

Geri Petito

"Jesus"

I'M NOT ASHAMED
TO PROCLAIM HIS NAME
I'M NOT ASHAMED
IT'S GOD I CLAIM!!

THE WORLD STIRS HATE
BUT GOD STIRS LOVE
THE WORLD'S LOST FAITH
IT'S FOUND UP ABOVE

THE WORLD SAYS GOD'S A MYTH
THE WORLD SAYS GOD IS FAKE
GOD SAYS I'M REALLY HERE
GOD SAYS I'M NO MISTAKE

THE LOST ARE BROKEN
THE BROKEN ARE LOST
CONDEMNING YOUR SOUL
NOT SPARING THE COST

GOD SAYS LISTEN
I'M HERE FOR YOU
JUST COME TO ME
I'LL MAKE YOU NEW

YOU LAUGH AT HIM
& CURSE HIS NAME
YOU DANCE WITH EVIL
IN THIS WAR GAME

RELIGION IS FALSE
AS FALSE AS CAN BE
WAS MADE BY MAN
AND NOT BY "HE"

RELIGION STILL HAS GOD
NAILED TO THAT CROSS
MAKING YOU THINK
THE CHURCH IS YOUR BOSS

WHEN JESUS SAID "IT IS FINISHED"
THEY TOOK HIM OFF THAT CROSS
HE ROSE FROM THE DEAD
SO YOUR SOUL WASN'T LOST

HE NO LONGER DANGLES
ON THE CROSS FROM THAT DAY
HE'S FREE FROM THAT CROSS
JESUS NOW MADE THE WAY

WE WEAR A CROSS
'CAUSE WE'RE HIS KID
TO BE REMINDED
WHAT THIS MAN DID

THE CRUCIFIX
SHOULD NOT BE WORN
RELIGION KEEPS GOD
ON THE CROSS AND SCORN

MAN MADE RULES
TO COST A FEE
THE PRICE OF JESUS
TO YOU IS FREE

COME AS YOU ARE
AND DON'T PRETEND
HE KNOWS ALL THINGS
BEGINNING TO END

RELIGION IS EVIL
IT'S CAUSED LOTS OF PAIN
GOD'S FULL OF LOVE
IN HEAVEN YOU'LL REIGN

RELIGION STARTS WARS
AND SPLITS UP THE HOME
THE YOUNG PEOPLE LEAVE
NOW LEFT TO JUST ROAM

RELIGION IS TOXIC
TAKE IT FROM ME
ALMOST COST ME MY LIFE
BUT GOD SET ME FREE

GROWING UP "CATHOLIC"
MADE ME HATE CHURCH
PRIESTS HURTING BOYS
MADE ME NOW SEARCH

I COULDN'T BELIEVE
GOD WAS IN THERE
TO ME CHURCH WAS EVIL
AND FILLED WITH DESPAIR

THEN I FOUND GOD
THE REAL ONE I MEAN
NOT STATUES ON CROSSES
BUT THE GOD I HAVE SEEN

I CRIED OUT ONE NIGHT
WHOEVER'S OUT THERE
PLEASE SHOW ME THE TRUTH
DOES ANYONE CARE?

IT WAS THEN I HEARD HIM
AS CLEAR AS CAN BE
I'M HERE..AND I CARE
I MADE YOU..FOR ME

YOU ARE NOT ALONE
I WILL LEAD THE WAY
I'LL NEVER LEAVE YOU
YOUR PRICE I DID PAY

I'LL PROTECT YOU & GUIDE YOU
AS LONG AS YOU WANT
TELL ME YOUR SORROWS
I'M YOUR CONFIDANT

I'M YOUR HEAVENLY FATHER
YOU'RE MY EARTHLY KID
THEIR WAS A PRICE ON YOU
TO THE HIGHEST OF BID

IT WAS THEN THAT I MARKED YOU
AND SAID YOU WERE MINE
I KNEW AT THAT MOMENT
YOU WERE MADE TO SHINE

I'LL NEVER PUT RULES
ON THE WAY YOU SHOULD LIVE
I GAVE YOU FREE WILL
FROM MY LIFE...I DID GIVE

YOU HAVE THE CHOICE
THE CHOICE IS YOURS
THEIR ARE 2 CHOICES
BEHIND EACH DOORS

ONE CHOICE IS DISTANT
AND IT WILL BRING PAIN
ONE CHOICE IS CLOSER
AND IT WILL BRING GAIN

THE CROSS I WAS NAILED TO
I WAS NAILED TO FOR YOU
NOT IN RELIGIONS NAME
IT WAS YOU...THAT I KNEW

SELF RIGHTEOUS WILL PAY
TRUST ME ON THIS
IF THEY EVER JUDGE YOU
THEM...I'LL DISMISS

EVERYONE SINS
THAT'S WHY I CAME
NO ONE IS BETTER
THAN YOU...IN MY NAME

SELF RIGHTEOUS WILL PERISH
I WON'T CALL THEM HOME
STAY HUMBLED AND LOYAL
IN HEAVEN YOU'LL ROAM

I CAN'T COME TO YOU
'TIL YOU LET ME IN
I'LL OPEN MY ARMS
& I'LL CLEANSE YOUR SIN

FATHER GOD I DO THANK YOU
FOR SENDING YOUR SON
TO SHED HIS BLOOD FOR ME
THEN HE SAID IT WAS DONE

HE SAID "IT IS FINISHED"
NOW LISTEN TO ME
HE NEVER SAID RELIGION
WOULD NOW SET YOU FREE

REMEMBER RELIGION
WAS NOT IN HIS PLAN
WHEN GOD SENT HIS SON
TO LIVE AS A MAN

THE PHARISEES & PRIESTS
WERE NOT LIVING RIGHT
THEY JUDGED & CONDEMNED
IN RELIGION WOULD FIGHT

GOD SAID ENOUGH
I'M SENDING YOU MY KID
TO TEACH YOU TO LOVE
EXPOSING SINS YOU HID

WHEN JESUS TOOK UP THE CROSS
HE DIED ON IT FOR YOU
YOU NOW NEED TO ACCEPT HIM
SO HE CAN MAKE U NEW

ASK HIM TO TAKE OVER
CAUSE YOU ARE WAY TO WEAK
I PROMISE...STRENGTH HE'LL GIVE YOU
IF ONLY JESUS YOU SEEK

"IT IS FINISHED"
WERE HIS LAST WORDS
HIS FLOCK WILL NOW BE SAVED
MARCHING... IN HERDS

"IT IS FINISHED"
I KNOW HE SAID
NOW YOU CAN LIVE
AND NOT BE DEAD

ASK JESUS TO FREE YOU
OF BONDAGE SATAN HOLDS
ASK JESUS TO STAND GUARD
AS THE BIBLE NOW UNFOLDS

ALL THAT WAS WRITTEN
IS BEING PLAYED OUT
WILL YOU BE READY
OR WILL YOU HAVE DOUBT

WILL YOU BE READY
THE DAY HE RETURNS
OR LEFT BEHIND
TO FEEL THE BURNS

MY PRAYER IS THIS
THAT YOU TAKE HEED
TO KNOW THE REASON
JESUS DID BLEED

THE TIME IS NEAR
IT REALLY IS
WILL YOU BE READY
TO SAY YOUR HIS?!

GERI 😇😈

I'm Not an Addict ... I'm Just an Ass!

Geri Petito

"Imagination Of Wonder"

I see pink skies
And fields of blues
Grassy Greens
And violet hues

I see clouds of cotton
And sands of gold
Crispy Colors
For me to hold

I see purple meadows
And oceans of wine
Chocolate fantasies
Not yours, but mine

Give me your hand
And i'll lead the way
So close your eyes
You're just visions away

This world is not yours
But you're welcome to stay
Imagination of wonder
Is what will take you away

GERI 😌

"Poet's Corner"

Do you have a place,
Where you like to go?
To sit & think...
Edgar Allen Poe?

One special place
Where no one else roams
Your special place
To read & write poems

Let your mind wander
Let your thoughts go
When your imagination is flying
Your paper will know

My Poet's Corner
Is filled with dreams
When the world is still
and yet it seems.....

When I think & write
When I dream & stare
When I play the part
I'm a Poet's pair

It can be in a room
Or under a tree
Your Poet's Corner
Is where you'll be

This quiet place
Is just for we few
The Poetry people
Me & You

I wander so far
Over shore & sea
I have a Treasure
I own the key!

<u>GERI</u>

MY CAT TIGER (1977)

I SAW A BAG JUST LYING THERE,
WITH PAPERS ALL INSIDE.
I KNEW IT'D BE A REAL SWELL PLACE,
FOR ME TO SIT AND HIDE.
I HEARD SOME STEPS, I SAW SOME FEET,
I FROZE & GOT ALL FLUSTERED.
MY HEART STOOD STILL, MY EYES ROLLED ROUND,
LOOKED UP AND HEARD "YOUR BUSTED."

BY: GERI

Geri Petito

"TIFFANY"

AS TIFFANY GREW UP
I LAUGHED & I CRIED
WATCHING HER GROW
MY JOY & MY PRIDE...

A GOOD LITTLE GIRL
EVERYONE SAID
BUT THEN CAME THE TEEN YEARS
THE YEARS WE ALL DREAD!

HER VOICE STARTED CHANGING
HER HEAD USED TO SPIN
GIVE ME STRENGHT ONE MORE DAY LORD
& PLEASE LET ME WIN!

HER ROOM WAS A MESS
HER FRIENDS WERE DERANGED
AND AS I SPEAK NOW
NONE OF THAT CHANGED...

HER ROOMS STILL A MESS
BUT HER FRIENDS I DO LUV
BUT MY KIDS HEART IS SO BIG
MUSTA COME FROM ABOVE!

SHE'S THE WARMEST & KINDEST
& TRUEST OF FRIEND
TO HELP U OR ME OUT
HER LAST DOLLAR SHE'LL SPEND..

A BETTER MOTHER
YOU WON'T FIND
SHE GIVES HER ALL
ONE OF A KIND

HER KIDS COME FIRST
THAT'S A FACT
THE LOVE SHE SHOWS
AINT NO ACT

SHE'D GO WITHOUT
BOTH FOOD & SLEEP
TO SEE THEIR SMILES
BOUNDS, SHE'D LEAP!

MY KID'S THE BEST
BETTER THAN ME
SHE SET THE RULES
HOW IT SHOULD BE

I LOVE MY KID
WITH ALL MY HEART
THIS KINDA LOVE
SETS US APART

NOT TO TOOT MY OWN HORN
THESE GREAT QUALITIES U SEE
EVERY LAST ONE OF THEM
SHE GOT THEM FROM ME!

ALL KIDDING ASIDE
I DO THANK MY GOD
I KNOW HE IS PLEASED
WITH HIS LOVING NOD

MOM

Geri Petito

MeMom's Baby's

CHRISTIAN & ARIA,
WHO NOW OWN MY HEART,
ALONG WITH MY DAUGHTER,
WHO PLAYS A BIG PART...

WHEN CHRISTIAN WAS BORN,
MY HEART SURE DID MELT,
I COULD NEVER EXPLAIN,
THESE FEELINGS I FELT...

WHEN I HAD MY TIFFANY,
I JUST NEVER KNEW,
I'D BE ABLE TO LUV,
NOT ONE BABE, BUT 2...

 MY HEART TOOK A BEATING,
LIKE NEVER BEFORE,
THIS BABY I NOW HOLD,
I COULD NEVER LUV MORE!

15 YRS. LATER ,
THINGS CHANGED NOW ONCE MORE,
MY KID BECAME A MOM ,
TO A LITTLE GIRL I ADORE!

ARIA..SHE NAMED HER,
THE DAY SHE WAS BORN,
IN GODS HANDS I PLACED HER,
MY HEART NOW IS TORN...

MY GRANDSON HAS A SISTER,
TO PROTECT & GUIDE HER THROUGH,
THE TRIALS & THE TRIBS,
THAT LIFE WILL BRING HER THROUGH...

TO LUV A 2ND GRANDKID,
THE WAY I LUV THE FIRST,
IMPOSSIBLE I THOUGHT IT'D BE,
BUT THEN, MY HEART JUST BURST!

THE AMOUNT OF LUV OUR HEARTS CAN HOLD,
THAT WE CAN NEVER SEE,
BUT ONCE I HELD THAT LITTLE BABE,
HER HEART JUST CAPTURED ME...

SO NOW I KNOW,THAT GOD MADE SURE,
THE AMOUNT OF KIDS DON'T MATTER,
EVERY TIME A NEW ONES BORN,
HE MAKES YOUR HEART MUCH FATTER...

ONCE MY EYES WERE LAID ON THEM,
LIFE JUST CAN'T GET NO BETTER,
I HAVE ENOUGH OF LUV TO GIVE,
NOW HERE IS YOUR LUV LETTER...

MeMom's HERE FOR ALL OF U,
HER LUV WILL NEVER DIE,
IN JESUS HANDS I'M PLACING U,
TO OUR FATHER IN THE SKY.

MeMom

I'm Not an Addict ... I'm Just an Ass!

The Faculty and Board of Managers of the

United Federation Of Cousins

certify to all that

Geraldine

has fulfilled the requirements of

The Board Of Cousins

and is hereby admitted the rights and privileges
belonging to that training and achievement
given under the Training Board seal. Unto her we provide the title of

World's Best Cousin.

July 15th, 2000

Signature

My Significant Other........

Looking back to find someone to assume the position of my significant other can be a great and tedious task. However for me it has been a time of great reflection into my past. So many people have touched my life, but who is the one true significant other. I was worried about hurting feelings with this paper, but I owe it to myself to be honest. I went with the most obvious choice, my favorite person. I realized I loved my great-aunt and she fits every other criteria but one, I can't talk to her about everything. So with that, it came to me who that one person was and I felt ridiculous for not getting it right away. But then I realized that it was okay that I not see it right away, because we don't always agree and she has to be a saint to put up with me and my mouth at times even my attitude but I figured out who my significant other is.

I was always forced to consider carefully what I said as a child up until probably fifteen years of age. I never knew who would hear it or whom I was talking to would tell. In essence I was always afraid and never told anyone how I felt or what I was actually thinking. And then things began to change. I met someone who would prove to be very special, someone who had always been there, but I had never seen before for whom she actually was. She brought me out of the miserable place that my mind was in. A place where everyone had some kind of motive for the way that they acted. Because, that's all it was an act. She brought me out of that dark place and to a place filled with light where happiness is all around. Over the years since I have become very close to her, and do not know what I would do without her. Probably without even knowing it, I used her guidance to help me through some very tight spots.

My cousin Geraldine _____ whom I call Jan is the only person I feel completely secure with. I can tell her anything and I know that she will be honest and help me make the best decisions. She has become my rock, someone for me to vent at and know I really don't mean it, and most of all she is my company in an otherwise empty life.

So when asked what a significant other is, this is how I respond. When your all alone and it seems like the whole world rest upon your shoulders, there is hope. When that loneliness burdens you down own your knees and you try out for help but amongst you there in silence, there is help. When you look around and see no one, there is someone. When you finally look up you will see someone with their arm extended approaching you. When they place their hand on your shoulder you know everything is going to be alright. That person is your significant other. When that person comforting was me she brought me up and showed me the grace of God and the good Lord Jesus, and for that I am eternally grateful. So, thank you Jan.

— Shaun Saffiell —

"The Friend I Found In You"

WHEN I ENTERED THIS WORLD, I WAS BORN WITH A FRIEND
LITTLE DID I KNOW,HOW CLOSE WE WOULD END
AS A BABY SHE HELD ME, AND SHE WATCHED ME GROW,
HELD ME CLOSE TO HER HEART,SO HER LOVE COULD FLOW...

AT THAT VERY MOMENT, OUR HEARTS BECAME ONE,
SHE CALLED ME "MOOK" & I CALLED HER "JUN"
LIVING CLOSE TO ME,ONLY 2 HOUSES DOWN,
MY COUSIN & ME, WERE FROM THE SAME TOWN...

LIFE HAD BROUGHT HER, THROUGH A TERRIBLE RACE,
BUT GERI WAS DELIVERED BY GODS LOVING GRACE,
MY COUSINS LIFE IS A WONDERFUL STORY,
FOR HER NAME NOW SITS IN THE BOOK OF GLORY!

THROUGH ALL OF LIFES TESTS,WHAT STILL HASN'T CHANGED,
IS THE BOND THAT WE SHARE,THAT GOD HAS ARRANGED,
I OFTEN WONDER, IF IT WEREN'T FOR JUN,
WHO WOULD I TURN TO, WHAT WOULD I HAVE DONE...

SHE UNDERSTANDS MY THOUGHTS & ALL MY EMOTIONS,
EASES MY PAIN,AND HER WORDS, ARE LIKE POTIONS,
WHENEVER I NEEDED HER, SHE WAS ALWAYS THERE,
TO GIVE ME HER LOVE,& HER FEELINGS TO SHARE...

NOW, I SHALL THANK HER, & SEND HER MY LOVE,
AND PRAY FOR HER PROTECTION,FROM OUR FATHER ABOVE
JUN...WE ARE COUSINS, AND OUR LOVE IS TRUE,
I THANK GOD FOR THE FRIEND...I FOUND IN YOU!

LOVE ALWAYS, "MOOK"...3/7/95

The Friend I Found In You!!
"From Jun To Mook"

WHEN U ENTERED THIS WORLD, U WERE BORN WITH A FRIEND,
I ABSOLUTELY KNEW, HOW CLOSE WE WOULD END...
AS A BABY, I HELD YOU, & I WATCHED YOU GROW,
HELD YOU CLOSE TO MY HEART, SO MY LOVE COULD FLOW...

AT THAT VERY MOMENT, OUR HEARTS BECAME ONE,
I CALLED U "MOOK" & U CALLED ME "JUN...
LIVING CLOSE TO ME, ONLY 2 HOUSES DOWN,
MY COUSIN & ME, WE'RE FROM THE SAME TOWN...

LIFE IS NOW BRINGING U, THROUGH A TERRIBLE RACE,
BUT MOOK, U WILLLL BE DELIVERED, BY GODS LOVING GRACE...
MY COUSINS LIFE NOW..IS A PAINFUL STORY,
BUT HIS NAME ABSOLUTELY ... ISSS IN...THE BOOK OF GLORY!

THROUGH ALL OF LIFES TESTS,WHAT STILL HASN'T CHANGED,
IS THE BOND THAT WE SHARE, THAT GOD HAS ARRANGED...
MOOK I OFTEN WONDER, IF IT WEREN'T FOR YOU,
BACK WHEN I WAS LOST...WHAT WOULD I HAVE DONE TOO...

I DO UNDERSTAND ALL YOUR THOUGHTS & EMOTIONS,
I WILL STILL EASE YOUR PAIN WITH MY GODLY POTIONS...
WHENEVER U NEED ME, I WILL ALWAYS BE THERE,
I WILL GIVE U MY LUV & I WILLLL ALWAYS CARE...

NOW ITS ME WHO THANKS GOD, FOR GIVING ME YOU,
MOOK WE ARE COUSINS, & OUR LOVE IS TRUE...
PROTECTION FROM OUR GOD I PRAY FOR U TOO,
I THANK GOD FOR THE FRIEND...I FOUND IN YOU!

I LOVE U, "JUN" 2016

GERI

I'm Not an Addict ... I'm Just an Ass!

Geri Petito

"ANT TURNS 40"

FORTY YEARS AGO
ON A STOOP IN N.Y. CITY
A BABY BOY WAS BORN
EATIN MEATBALLS & "SPAGHITTY"

IN ONE HAND WAS HIS BOTTLE
IN THE OTHER A PIECE OF BREAD
AS HIS MOTHER FED HIM
"THAT'S ENOUGH" HIS FATHER SAID!

HIS SISTER WAS NEGLECTED
SHE WAS SKINNY AS A BONE
EVEN HER BABY BOTTLE
HE TOOK & MADE HIS OWN!

AS THIS LITTLE BOY GREW OLDER
HIS SCHOOL DAYS WEREN'T FUN
ONE COLD & SNOWY MORNIN'
HE WAS DRAGGED IN, BY A "NUN"

SISTER MARY JOSEPH
DRAGGED ANT ACROSS THE FLOOR
THE ONE SHE DIDN'T NOTICE
WAS MOM OUTSIDE THE DOOR!

NOT EVEN A HUNDRED HAIL MARY'S
COULD HAVE SAVED THAT NUN THAT DAY
LUCY DRAGGED HER BY HER HAIR
AND ALL SHE COULD DO WAS PRAY!

NOW HERE WE ARE YEARS LATER
SOME THINGS HAVE REMAINED THE SAME
ANTHONY IS STILL THE ONE
WHO THINKS, "DON CORLEONE'S" HIS NAME

EVEN FROM HIS HOSPITAL BED
BUSINESS WAS CONDUCTED
ANYONE WHO CAME HIS WAY
WAS VIRTUALLY INSTRUCTED

JUN DO THIS, MICHAEL JON DO THAT
AND TIFFANY, YOU COME HERE
FEED ME, RUB ME, SHAVE ME, SCRUB ME
FOR WE WERE ALL FILLED WITH FEAR!

MOM AND DAD, DON'T COME TODAY
FOR "JUN" IS HERE TO STAY
I'D RATHER HAVE "HER" CLEAN MY BUTT
SO THE NURSES STAY AWAY

LEE LEE COME & SIT BY ME
IN CASE I NEED A SNACK
BY THE WAY, YOU DO LOOK BORED
YOU WANNA RUB MY BACK?

CHICKY DO THIS & CHICKY DO THAT
JUNIOR COME RUB MY FEET
TELL MOMMY & BOIN TO COOK FOR ME
AND BRING ME LOTS TO EAT!

ALL KIDDING ASIDE, WE MUST EXPRESS
HOW THANKFUL WE ARE TODAY
THAT GOD HAS PUT YOU IN OUR LIVES
AND SPARED YOUR LIFE THAT DAY

ANYONE HERE WHO KNOWS YOU
WILL NEVER DISAGREE
THE BIGGEST HEART, THE'LL EVER FIND
IS IN YOU...ANTHONY!

I'LL NOW ASK GOD TO PROTECT YOU
KEEP YOU SAFE IN HIS ARMS TO STAY
WE THANK YOU JUST FOR BEING YOU
GOD BLESS U ON YOUR BIRTHDAY!

LUV "JUN"

A PIECE OF OUR BLOCK IS GONE; R.I.P. MOM

AS FAR AS I CAN REMEMBER
& FOR THE LAST 30 YEARS
OUR STREET HAS SHARED LAUGHTER
& ALSO SHED TEARS...

7 HOUSES SHARED
OUR FAMILY STANDS STRONG
BUT TODAY WE SAY GOODBYE
NOW A PIECE OF OUR BLOCK IS GONE...

MY AUNT LOO WILL B REMEMBERED
SHE WAS THE QUEEN OF OUR STREET
 BUT THIS YEAR ON THE HOLIDAYS
WILL BE AN EMPTY SEAT...

I WON'T LET HER GO
WITHOUT SHARING SOME JOY
AND THINKING OF THE MEMORIES
GROWING UP AS A BOY...

WE ALL KNEW AUNT LOO
BY THE WORDS SHE WOULD YELL
THE WHOLE BLOCK COULD HEAR HER
JERRY....U GO TO HELL!

HE PLAYED BACCI EACH NITE
UNTIL DINNER WAS DONE
WHEN HE HEARD AUNT LOO YELL
U SHOULD SEE JERRY RUN!

I'M COMIN' LOO
AS HE RAN THROUGH THE YARD
IF HE WASN'T THERE ON TIME
HE'D GET SMACKED REALLY HARD!

AUNT LOO WOULD COOK FOR AN ARMY
CAUSE ON OUR STREET U CAN'T TELL
WHO WOULD BRING OVER COMPANY
OR WHO'D RING OUR BELL!

SHE WOULD TAKE IN STRAY ANIMALS
& THE DOGS JUN WOULD GIVE AWAY
AS UNCLE JERRY SHOOK HIS HEAD
WITH NOTHING ELSE TO SAY...

SHE SENT MONEY TO AFRICA
TO HELP THOSE IN NEED,
OR HELP ANYONE IN TROUBLE
JUST TO DO A GOOD DEED!

ALL HER YELLING & SCREAMING
SHOULD BE SET APART,
FOR MY AUNT LUCY
HAD A REALLY BIG HEART!

SHE WORE HER HEART ON HER SLEEVE
& U WOULD KNOW RITE AWAY
IF SHE DID NOT LIKE YOU
BOY....THE THINGS SHE WOULD SAY!

SHE ACCEPTED EVERYONE UNCONDITIONALLY
BLACK, WHITE, OR GAY
ALL WERE WELCOMED IN HER HOUSE
SHE HAD HER OWN SPECIAL WAY!

SHE LUVD HER 2 CHILDREN
EVEN IF SHE WOULD YELL
INSIDE WAS A GOOD PERSON
I SURELY COULD TELL

TIFFANY & CHRISTIAN
WERE THE JOY OF HER HEART
LET US ALL REMEMBER HER
FOR NOW SHE MUST PART...

AUNT LUCY WE LUV U
YOU'LL BE MISSED ON OUR STREET
BUT DON'Y U WORRY
FOR ONE DAY WE WILL MEET!

WE WILL NEVER 4GET YOU
OUR FAMILY STAYS STRONG
EVEN THOUGH ON THIS DAY
A PIECE OF OUR BLOCK IS GONE!

GERI & MOOK!

"TILL WE MEET AGAIN"

A FAREWELL TO U DAD,
BUT I NEED U TO KNOW,
WHEN GOD GAVE ME U DAD,
U CAME WRAPPED WITH A BOW..

YOUR ENTIRE LIFE,
THAT U HAD ONCE LED,
WAS ALL FOR YOUR FAMILY,
LIKE U ALWAYS SAID...

A MORE SELFLESS MAN,
THERE NEVER CAN BE,
WHAT U DID FOR US DAD,
WE ALL NOW DO SEE...

TO MY KID & MY GRANDKIDS,
NO WORDS CAN EXPLAIN,
THE LUV THAT U GAVE THEM,
PLUS FINANCIAL GAIN...

THE DAY THEY WERE BORN
YOUR HEART TOOK A HIT
MY KIDS THEY NOW OWNED U
YOUR LUV NEVER QUIT

I STILL THINK TO THIS DAY,
WHAT DID I EVER DO,
FOR GOD TO HAVE BLESSED ME,
WITH A FATHER LIKE U...

YOUR SON IS A COPY
OF THE MAN U ONCE WERE
A MEDAL OF HONOR I GIVE U
& A BIG THANK U SIR

MY MOTHER WAS LUCKY
TO HAVE HAD SUCH A MAN
U GAVE HER 2 KIDS
IT WAS ALL IN GODS PLAN

I KNEW ANT WAS MOMS FAVE
BUT I DIDNT CARE
I KNEW I WAS YOURS
SO THAT MADE IT FAIR!

DAD PLAYED BACCI EACH NITE
UNTILL DINNER WAS DONE
WHEN HE HEARD MY MOM YELL
U SHOULD SEE MY DAD RUN

I'M COMIN' LOO
AS HE RAN THROUGH THE YARD
IF HE WASN'T ON TIME
HE'D GET SMACKED REALLY HARD!

U ACCEPTED EVERYONE UNCONDITIONALLY
BLACK, WHITE, OR GAY
ALL WERE WELCOMED IN OUR HOME
TO EAT OR SLEEP ANY DAY

I SURE DROVE U CRAZY
MOST OF MY LIFE
NO MATTER WHAT I DID
U TOOK IT IN STRIFE

I BROUGHT HOME STRAY PETS
& STRAY PEOPLE TOO
U JUS SHOOK YOUR HEAD
& SAID WHAT THE HECK DID U DO

AN EXCITING LIFE
U SURE DID LEAD
I FOLLOWED IN YOUR STEPS
U PLANTED THE SEED

INDEPENDENCE U TAUGHT ME
& TO ALWAYS STAND TOUGH
I TAKE AFTER U DAD
EVEN WHEN IT GETS ROUGH

U TAUGHT ME TO LUV
& RESPECT ALL MANKIND
TO FEED ALL THE HUNGRY
& HELP WHO'S BEHIND

I THANK GOD FOR THAT MOMENT,
WHEN WE SHARED HOW WE FEEL,
I TOLD U I LUVD U,
& U KEPT IT REAL...

YOUR WORDS THAT U SAID,
I'LL NEVER FORGET,
U SAID I'M AMAZING,
THE BEST U HAD MET...

I THANKED U THEN,
WITH ALL MY HEART,
& SAID I'M SO SORRY,
WE WILL SOON HAVE TO PART...

THE BEST MEMORY I HAVE
IN THE TOMB JESUS LAID
U ACCEPTED THE LORD
IT WAS THEN THAT U PRAYED

I KNEW FROM THAT MOMENT
ID BE WORRY FREE
I KNOW YOUR WITH JESUS
AND ONE DAY... YOU'LL SEE ME

EVEN YOUR DEATH
IT HOLDS SOMETHING GREAT
40 YEARS AGO TO THE DAY
YOUR PAPPA MET HIS FATE

GOD SAID IT'S TIME,
MY DAD HADDA GO
THE ONE THING FOR SURE
HE'S IN HEAVEN..I KNOW

WHEN I GET TO HEAVEN
THE PARTY WILL START
ELVIS WILL BE SINGING
HOW GREAT THOU ART!

I LUV U DAD !

Notes

Notes

_____

_____

_____

_____

_____

_____

_____

_____

_____

_____

_____

_____

_____

_____

_____

_____

_____

_____

_____

_____

Chapter 19

"My Book Aint For Wimps"

Four years ago when my book was first published, I received a message saying they bought my book and felt it was too much of a "Tough Love" for their child at the time. That inspired me to have a You Tube video titled "My Book Aint For Wimps" which is public. Once They decided their loved one was ready for my book, I became the family's recovery coach. God is good, and brough healing to them through me.

Geri Petito

My Book Aint For Wimps

I'M NOT AN ADDICT...I'M JUST AN ASS!
IS THE TITLE OF MY BOOK...
ONLY IF YOU'RE NOT A WIMP...
OPEN IT & TAKE A LOOK!

MY BOOK'S MAKIN' HEADLINES
MY BOOK;S TURNIN' HEADS
MY BOOK'S CAUSIN' PEOPLE
TO STOP TAKIN' MEDS!

MY BOOK'S NOT FOR ALL OF U
MY BOOK'S WAY TO REAL
IF U DARE TO OPEN IT
MIGHT CAUSE U TO FEEL!

OMG...NOT FEELINGS
CAUSE THEN I MIGHT JUST CRACK
IF I DON'T NUMB MY BRAIN
THERE WILL BE NO TURNING BACK!

MY BOOK AINT FOR WIMPS
ITS NOT FOR THE WEAK
MY BOOK'S FOR THE STRONG
IF BEING SOBER U SEEK!

MY BOOK AINT FOR WIMPS
NOT FOR BABYS WHO WHINE
MY BOOK AINT FOR WIMPS
IT'S FOR THOSE WITH A SPINE!

SO DON'T B A BABY
DON'T B A FOOL
IF U R AN ADDICT
THEN U R NOT COOL!

MY BOOK AINT FOR WIMPS
IT'S NOT FOR THE SCARED
MY BOOK AINT FOR WIMPS
IT'S FOR THE DESPAIRED!

IF SELF PITY U DO SEEK
SYMPATHY IS YOUR FRIEND
STANDING ON UR OWN 2 FEET?
NOPE...ON OTHERS U DEPEND!

U GO THROUGH LIFE WOE IS ME,
SORROW & PITY U PREFER
RESPONSIBILITY U REFUSE TO TAKE
YOUR LIFE IS NOW A BLUR!

MY BOOK AINT FOR WIMPS
IT MIGHT MAKE U CLEAN
UNLESS U LIKE USING
& REMAINING A TEEN!

U AINT THE ONE
WHO HASTA DECIDE
IT'S YOUR INNER SELF
& YOUR STUPID PRIDE!

MY CHALLENGE IS THIS
TO ALL WHO APPLY
READ MY BOOK & GET CLEAN
THE LIMIT'S....THE SKY!

SO LET'S NOT CONFUSE
WHAT I GOTTA SAY
CAUSE U DO HAVE A CHOICE
U SHOULD MAKE IT TODAY!

MY BOOK AINT FOR WIMPS
WIMPS NEED NOT APPLY
THE ONES THAT WILL READ IT
WILL B NATURALLY HIGH!

GERI 😚

"Unlikeliness Of Love"

THE UNLIKELINESS OF LOVE
TO ME IS REALLY RARE
LIFE SOMETIMES THROWS US CURVES
LIFE SOMETIMES SEEMS UNFAIR

BUT WE DO GET BACK
WHAT WE PUT OUT
LET'S B POSITIVE
DON'T LIVE WITH DOUBT

THE YEAR IS 2018
AS I LOOK BACK
COMPASSION & UNITY
IS WHAT WE LACK

JUDGING & RUDENESS
RACIST & GREED
LACKING RESPECT
WE SEEM TO BREED

WHERE IS THE LOVE
WE SHOULD B SHOWING
WHERE IS THE LOVE
WE SHOULD B KNOWING

WE LOOK FOR LOVE
IN ALL THE WRONG PLACES
LOVE SHOULD B SHINING
IN EVERYONE'S FACES

Geri Petito

A BABY IS BORN
NOT KNOWING HATE
THAT THERE IS TAUGHT
& NEEDS TO DEFLATE

THEN AS ADULTS
WE DON'T KNOW OUR WORTH
HURT PEOPLE, HURT PEOPLE
ALL OVER THIS EARTH

SOMETIMES LOVE FINDS US
I HOPE THAT IT DOES
LOVE CURES ALL
& CLEARS UP THAT FUZZ

U CAN'T LOVE ANOTHER
'TILL U LOVE U FIRST
ONCE U CAN DO THAT
YOUR HEART WILL THEN BURST

THE MAN IN THE MIRROR
HE SPEAKS THE TRUTH
PLEASE STOP SEEKING
THAT FOUNTAIN OF YOUTH

HAPPINESS DOES NOT LIE
WITHIN YOUR YOUTH & LOOKS
IT'S NOT IN MONEY OR THINGS
OR EVEN IN HAND BOOKS

IF U CAN LOOK HIM IN THE EYE
& SLEEP AT NIGHT IN PEACE
THEN U KNOW U HAVE ARRIVED
HAPPINESS... WILL INCREASE

OUR VALUES GOT LOST
COMMON SENSE DISAPPEARED
OUR MORALS GOT TAINTED
TWISTED & FEARED

NOT SURE WHAT'S HAPPENED
BUT LET'S GET ON TRACK
HELPING EACH OTHER
BROWN, RED, WHITE OR BLACK

WE ALL DO CRAVE LOVE
THAT'S HOW WE WERE MADE
EVIL BROUGHT IN HATE
OUR GOODNESS, SWAYED

A HEALTHY OUTLOOK
BEGINS WITH U
A LIFE FULFILLED
IS UP TO U TOO...

MAINTAIN A BALANCE
IN ALL THAT U DO
YOUR SANITY MY FRIEND
IS ALL UP TO U

OUR RELATIONSHIPS...OUR JOBS
FINANCES & OUR VIEWS
CONTENTMENT IN OUR LIVES
DEPENDS ON WHAT WE CHOOSE

SO KNOW YOUR WORTH
IT ALL STARTS THERE
SOME USE MEDITATION
OTHERS USE PRAYER

YOU ARE IN CHARGE
OF LIFE CHOICES U MAKE
KEEPING THEM HEALTHY
IS YOUR JOURNEY TO TAKE

SO PUT ON A SMILE
& FAKE IT AT FIRST
I PROMISE U THIS
A "REAL SMILE" WILL BURST!

IF YOUR LOOKING TO FIND
WHAT LIFE'S DESTINED TO BE
ITS ALL UP TO U FRIEND
BECAUSE U OWN THE KEY!

GERI ☺

"A Peace of Mind"

FROM MY HEART
TO MY MOUTH
THESE WORDS
I WILL SHOUT!

WOMAN & MEN
R JUST NOT THE SAME
IT'S REALLY UNFAIR
TO PLAY THE SAME GAME

WE THINK WITH OUR HEARTS
THEY THINK WITH THEIR HEADS
YOU HEARD ME RIGHT
IN THEIR MINDS & BEDS

I DON'T LET THEM HURT ME
IT'S NOT THEIR FAULT
A SWITCH IN THEIR BRAINS
JUST COMES TO A HAULT

WE DO NOT HAVE
THAT SWITCH AT ALL
BUT LISTEN LADIES
WE STILL STAND TALL

AS WE MATURE
WE DO LEARN WHAT'S RITE
WE DO HAVE THE POWER
TO NOW... "FIGHT OR FLIGHT"

MOST MEN THINK AT TIMES
THE LOVE THAT THEY SHOW
IS ENOUGH TO SUSTAIN
WHILE WE'RE THINKING...NO!

NOT ALWAYS THEIR FAULT
THEY DO LEARN FROM US
IF WE WANT THEM TO CHANGE
SHOWING LOVE IS A MUST

THEY NEED GREAT RESPECT
IT'S HOW THEY ARE MADE
RESPECT FILLED WITH LOVE
GROUND RULES ARE THEN LAID

WE HAVE THE CHOICE
LADIES HEAR ME
IF WE'RE NOT RESPECTED
THEN SET HIM FREE!

A WOMAN NEEDS
TO BE HEARD
& VALIDATED
BY HIS WORD

IF A MAN SHOWS LOVE
WE GIVE IT BACK
WE MUST FEEL SAFE
OR LOVE WE LACK

IF YOU GIVE A WOMAN
LOVE OR HATE
YOU WILL GET IT BACK
10 FOLDS...JUST WAIT!

ONCE WE REALLY
"KNOW OUR WORTH"
OTHERS ACTIONS
TOWARDS US...WON'T HURT

OUR HEARTS WE WEAR
FOR ALL TO SEE
IT INTIMIDATES MEN
BUT SETS US FREE

A MAN HAS BOXES
HE STORES STUFF
WE HAVE JUST ONE
IT HOLDS ENOUGH

THEY CAN SEPERATE
THROUGH THE DAY
WOMAN WERE MADE
KEEPING ALL AT BAY

LADIES KNOW THIS
YOU DO HAVE THE POWER
TO CHOOSE MEN WISELY
TO WATER YOUR FLOWER

MY HEAVENLY FATHER
& EARTHLY ONE
CREATED ME STRONG
NOT WEAK & UNDONE

I DO LOVE OUR MEN
LADIES HEAR THIS
WHEN THEY R TRYING
THAT...DON'T DISMISS

IT'S NO LONGER A MANS WORLD
I'VE JUST PROVED THAT
WE MUST WORK TOGETHER
MEN & WOMAN FORMAT!

LIFE COULD BE GREAT
IT'S IN OUR HANDS
MEN & WOMAN UNITE
IN ALL THE LANDS!

LAST BUT NOT LEAST
MEN SHOULD TIP THEIR HAT
'CAUSE WOMAN ARE STRONGER
VAGINAS PROVE THAT!

GERI 😛

Healthy Outlook

A HEALTHY OUTLOOK
BEGINS WITH U
A LIFE FULFILLED
IS UP TO U TOO...

A HEALTHY DIET
IS WHERE U START
BUT A HEA;LTHY MIND
IS THE MAJOR PART

YOUR THOUGHTS R WIRED
TO MAKE U THINK
BUT WHAT U DO
CAN MAKE U SINK

SO KEEP ALL YOUR THOUGHTS
UPLIFTING & REAL
FEEDING YOUR MIND CRAP
WILL DESTROY THE WAY U FEEL

MUSIC IS SAID TO
DEFINE WHO U R
THE KIND U R LISTENING TOO
REALLY MATTERS BY FAR...

UPBEAT N POSITIVE
R THE NOTES U SHOULD HEAR
NOTHING WITH VIOLENCE
OR YOU'LL LIVE IN FEAR

MUSIC IS A MUST
FOR U TO KEEP YOUR JOY
ESPECIALLY IF ITS ELVIS
CAUSE ELVIS IS MY BOY!

GERI

Notes

_____

_____

_____

_____

_____

_____

_____

_____

_____

_____

_____

_____

_____

_____

_____

_____

_____

_____

_____

Notes

_____

_____

_____

_____

_____

_____

_____

_____

_____

_____

_____

_____

_____

_____

_____

_____

_____

_____

_____

_____

Chapter 20

"MsNiteOwl Poker"

I'm not only a poker player, I'm also a poker dealer. I owned a league for about ten years, in Mercer County NJ called MsNiteOwl Poker. My poker league was significant part of my life for a very long time. I was in bars and restaurants almost every night with this league, and guess what? I never had the urge to pick up. The difference between me and most addicts is simple I'm not allowing the system to brain wash me into believing I have the disease of addiction which I'm powerless over. My philosophy is I am not powerless over anything, I do not have a disease and today I am "CHOOSING" to live a clean a sober life. Most importantly I'm choosing to live a healthy, productive, successful, and fulfilled life. I promise you this, so can you. The key to a happy life is to forever break the stigma of "Bondage". I may be repeating myself but the percentage of addicts staying clean and sober is extremely low.

In a 2010 study 109 addicts were studied during and after drug addiction. The percentage of relapse was quite high with 91% relapsing. Here's the good news, you can be one of the exceptions just as I am. The answer is simple. Choose to not pick up, remove all sugar from your diet, choose healthy food options, get a healthy support system, and ask God to come into your life.

The first step before doing any of these things is to look in the mirror and say to yourself

"I'M WORTH IT".

One of the sayings I teach my clients is "K.Y.W." Know Your Worth!

MsNiteOwl POKER

MsNiteOwl POKER
IS THE BEST LEAGUE IN TOWN...
IT COST U NO FEE
TO PUSH ME AROUND!

U WIN NITELY PRIZES
& QUARTERLY TOO
U EVEN GET CHIPPED UP
IF U BRING SOMEONE NEW!

SO CHECK OUT MY WEBSITE
THE SAME AS MY NAME
MOSTLY IN MERCER COUNTY
U CAN PLAY AT ANY GAME!

THE BRASS RAIL IN MONMOUTH
ON TUESDAYS WERE THERE
A GREAT GAME I TELL U
IF U SUCK THEY WON'T CARE!

A POINTER I'LL GIVE U...
& TRUST ME, IT'S TRUE....
WHEN U SEE 2 ACES
NOT MUCH U COULD DO!

U THINK THEY R AWESOME
N YOUR GONNA WIN
ACES WILL DESTROY U
THEY'LL END UP IN THE BIN!

DO U WANNA KNOW THE BEST HAND
THAT U COULD EVER PLAY
ILL TELL U NOW MY SECRET
J4 IS THE HAND TO PLAY!

OTHERS WON'T BELIEVE
THEY'LL LAUGH AT U & SAY
U GOTTA BE AN IDIOT
THROW THOSE 2 CARDS AWAY!

A MAN USED TO OWN THIS
WAY BACK IN THE DAY
NITEOWL POKER
WE ALL WOULD SAY...

BUT NOW A FEMALE
HAS CHANGED THE NAME
SHE ADDED THE Ms,
& PUT THE BOYZ TO SHAME!

GOIN ON 8 YRS.
WERE PROUD TO B HERE
WE WANNA THANK ALL OUR PLAYERS
WHO PLAY YEAR AFTER YEAR!

GERI 😋

J4 Baby!!

TEXAS HOLD'EM IS REALLY HUGE
THIS KINDA GAME BRINGS MANY FOOLS
POCKET ACES...THEY DO SUCK
BUT J4 IS THE HAND THAT RULES!

PLAYING POKER HAS MANY SIDES
SOMETIMES WE WIN & MAKE IT BIG
& SOMETIMES WE LOSE OUR SHIRTS......
POKER PLAYERS THINK THEY'RE GREAT
WINNING BIG MAKES US FEEL GOOD
BUT WHEN WE LOSE...DAMM IT HURTS!

NOT QUITE SURE THE REASONS WHY
WE LUV TO SIT & PLAY
DEGENERATES...I THINK WE ARE
LOOKING AT CARDS ALL NITE & DAY

WE SIT IN A CHAIR FOR HOURS
& SOMETIMES EVEN FOR DAYS
LOOKIN AT CARDS & PONDERING PLAY
DO WE ...HOLD EM...FOLD EM...OR RAISE

ME & BIG RICKY R BUDDIES
POKER DEALERS...WE BOTH BECAME
BUT PLAYING POKER'S OUR PASSION
WE EAT, SLEEP & BREATH THE GAME!

RICKY WOULD RATHER HAVE PAIRS
CONNECTORS I'D RATHER SEE
PAIRS ONLY HAVE 2 OUTS
SILLY BOY...JUS LISTEN TO ME!

6,7 & 7,8 I LUV
J,10 IS REALLY THE BEST
IMAGINE THEM BEING SUITED
PUT YOUR OPPONENTS TO DA TEST!

I'D ALWAYS RAISE WITH HANDS LIKE THESE
I'D NEVER FOLD OR JUS CALL
PREFLOP I THINK THEY'RE GOLDEN
PLAY IT RITE...DON'T DROP DA BALL

U CAN RAISE OPPONENTS OFF
BY NEVER ACTING WEAK
YOUR CARDS DON'T REALLY MATTER
ACTING STRONG WILL MAKE THEM FREAK

THIS GAME IS NOT FOR ALL OF U
BLUFFING IS PART OF IT ALL
FOLDING & RAISING IS NEEDED
BUT SOMETIMES U JUS GOTTA CALL

PEOPLE WHO DO NOT PLAY POKER
CAN'T REALLY IMAGINE THE THRILL
OF WATCHING THE CHIPS BEING PASSED
& THINKING IT'S ALL DONE WITH SKILL

SUM ARGUE IT'S ALL MOSTLY LUCK
& SUM SAY IT'S JUS A DUMB GAME
WHO REALLY CARES WHAT'S DA TRUTH
WE'RE HOPING 4 FORTUNE & FAME!

POKER PLAYERS HAVE BECOME OUR IDOLS
NEGREANU, IVEY & PHIL
THESE PLAYERS ARE 3 OF THE BEST...
WE ALL INSPIRE TO BE THEM
& THINK WE'RE AS GOOD AS THE REST!

THE CRAZY THING ABOUT US FOOLS
ITS REALLY NOT THE MONEY
EVEN WHEN WE WIN ALOT
WE PLAY TILL WE LOSE...HOW FUNNY

GERI 😉

Notes

_____

_____

_____

_____

_____

_____

_____

_____

_____

_____

_____

_____

_____

_____

_____

_____

_____

_____

_____

Notes

_____

_____

_____

_____

_____

_____

_____

_____

_____

_____

_____

_____

_____

_____

_____

_____

_____

Chapter 21

"Radio Shows"

Imagine being invited to be interviewed for my book four years ago, and then having the honor to host my own show. That's when this all started.

The Geri Petito Show

IMAGINE THAT...
I HAD 5 SHOWS...
I CAN'T BELIEVE
IT WAS ME, THEY CHOSE

FIRST HAMILTON RADIO
THEN ON PANJ
ON VINNIES SHOW I MET ROB BELL
I JOINED WITH THEM THAT DAY!

DOC G STARTED THIS
IT'S ALL BECAUSE OF U
ASKING ME TO COME ALONG
SOMETHING I HADDA DO

BROTHER O WATCHED MY SHOWS
& SAID PLEASE COME ALONG
IF YOU DO...I PROMISE
WITH ME...U CAN'T GO WRONG!

BEVERLY NATION ONLINE
TALKSHOE RADIO, MAKE WAY
ONCE YOU GET ME STARTED
I'LL HAVE SO MUCH TO SAY!

BROTHER O INFORMED ME
MY SHOWS ARE FLYING HIGH
NOW ON DAMON NETWORK
"D.A.M.O.N LOOKS" WILL REACH THE SKY!

I WAS EVEN NAMED
"THE JERSEY JEWEL"
BY BROTHER "O"
DAMM, THAT'S COOL!

MY NICKNAME ON
THE OTHER SHOWS
GERI THE SMARTASS
CAUSE OF MY LOGOS

NOW PICKED UP BY MY 5TH ONE
OWNED BY BARB & STEVE
REMEMBER THEN RADIO
ALL OLDIES I BELIEVE

LARRY CHANCE & THE EARLS
THEIR SONG "REMEMBER THEN"
THIS STATION IS NAMED AFTER
NOW LARRY IS MY FRIEND!

I CAN'T BELIEVE THE CALL
GOOD NEWS FROM ME TO YOU
AN AWARD OUT OF GERMANY
MY ACHIEVEMENTS, IT'S TRUE

U WON'T BELIEVE THIS
I SWEAR TO YOU IT'S TRUE
NOW A NOMINEE 4 HALL OF FAME
ALONG WITH BROTHER O...WHO KNEW?!

WHAT A RIDE
THIS REALLY HAS BEEN
CAN'T WAIT TO HEAR
BROTHER O & I WIN!!

BUT EVEN IF
IT DON'T HAPPEN
BEIN' NOMINATED
CREATED CLAPPIN'!

OMG WE GOT THAT CALL
TO TELL US THAT WE'D WIN?
BROTHER O & I MADE IT...
WE WERE INDUCTED IN!!

INTERNATIONAL HALL OF FAMERS
FOREVER ENSHRINED WE'LL BE
INTERNET D.J FOR BROTHER O
INTERNET RADIO HOST FOR ME!

THE BEST PART OF THE CEREMONY
BOTH OUR CHILDREN GAVE A SPEECH
ON BEHALF OF THEIR PARENTS
PROUD OF ALL THE SOULS WE'D REACH

FOR THOSE WHO KNOW ME
& THOSE WHO DON'T
TO KEEP ME SILENT
U CAN'T...U WON'T!

MY SHOW WILL B
TO KEEP IT REAL
ON HOW I SEE IT
& HOW I FEEL...

TO TELL THE TRUTH...
& XPOSE THE LIES
GET OUT OF THE DARK
LET'S OPEN OUR EYES

IF U WANNA GET HEALTHY
OR LEARN HOW TO LIVE
JUS LISTEN TO ME THEN
INSPIRATION I GIVE!

IF ADDICTIONS YOUR STRUGGLE
NO MATTER WHICH ONE
I WROTE THE BOOK ON ADDICTION
THAT BATTLE I'VE WON!

I'M NOT AN ADDICT
I'M JUST A ASS
IS THE TITLE OF MY BOOK...
SO CHECK IT OUT
U WONT REGRET
THE MINUTE U TAKE A LOOK!!

BUT ALOT OF INFO
I SURE DO KNOW
SO TUNE IN & LEARN STUFF
ON THE "Geri Petito" SHOW !

GERI 😉

Geri Petito

My Radio Jingle!!

I'm not an addict.
I'm just an ass.
and in time, this too shall pass.
I'm not an addict.
I'm just an ass.
Life's a teacher
take the class.
I'm not an addict.
I'm just an ass.
Love's the answer
Greener grass
I'm not an addict.
I'm just an ass.
one day a time
Free at last!!

We're not powerless.
Over addiction.
hear me now.
it's truth not fiction.

When you don't know.
just what to do.
if what you're feeling.
is really true.
just keep your ideas.
safe and sound.
that's exactly how change is found.

I'm not an addict.
I'm just an ass.
and in time, this too shall pass.
I'm not an addict.
I'm just an ass.
Life's a teacher
take the class.
I'm not an addict.
I'm just an ass.
Love's the answer
Greener grass
I'm not an addict.
I'm just an ass.
one day a time
Free at last!!

"WHITE GIRLZ CAN RAP"

I Was Told Not To Try It Wit My Stuff
U Jus A Poet, Aint good Enough
I Said Wait A Minute, Hold Up, Yoo...Yoo
Jus 'Cause I'm White, Somthin' U Gotta Know
White Girlz Can Jump & White Girlz Can Tap
White Girlz Can FreeStyle & White Girlz Can Rap
I'm Here To Show Ya We Got It Too
Hold On To Your Seat, I Got Somethin' To Do
My Rapper Friends, Please Take A Bow
I'm Here To Show U How I Do It Now
I Luv Your Style, I Got You're Back
This White Girl Is Hot, She Probly Half Black
To All Of U Out There I Jus Gotta Say
Today Is The First Day I'm Rappin This Way
Times Have Been Trying For All Of Us Here
This World Is In Need Of Alotta Prayer
Let's Come Together & Pray As One
Put Color Aside, 'Cause Of What Christ Done
He Sees No Color, He Sees No Rank
He Gave His Life, That Wasn't A Prank
The Times R Scary & Filled With Despair
I'm Here To Tell Ya, That Our God Can Hear
He Hears All Your Sorrows & Troubles My Friend
He'll Never Forsake U, Not Now 'Till The End
I'm Just A Messenger To Tell The World
Jus Give It To God, His Love Has Been Hurled
Jesus Said "It Is Finished" & I'll Say It Too
This White Girl Can Rap, She Dropped The Mic On U!

GERI

"I'm An Author!"

TO BE A WRITER
OUT OF THE BOX U MUS THINK
U NEED TO BECOME
THAT ONE MISSING LINK

LET YOUR MIND WANDER
& LET YOUR THOUGHTS GO
WHEN YOUR IMAGINATION IS FLYING
YOUR PAPER WILL KNOW...

MY POETS CORNER IS FILLED WITH DREAMS
WHEN THE WORLD IS STILL, & YET IT SEEMS
WHEN I THINK & WRITE WHEN I DREAM & STARE
WHEN I PLAY THE PART I'M A POETS PAIR

FOR U TO MAKE MAGIC
WITH YOUR PAPER & PEN
GET INTO YOUR THOUGHTS
AGAIN & AGAIN

DON'T B AFRAID
TO REALLY STEP OUT
U GOTTA TELL THE WORLD
WHAT UR THINKIN ABOUT

LEFT BRAINED WE'RE NOT
I'M SURE YOU'LL AGREE
THAT LOGICAL CRAP
IT'S JUS NOT FOR WE

WE'D RATHER PAINT
& DRAW & WRITE
IT KEEPS US HAPPY
CHEERY & BRIGHT

IF YOU'RE NOT CREATIVE
OR JUS DON'T KNOW HOW
JUS PULL OUT YOUR PAD
& START WRITING NOW!!

GERI

Notes

_____

_____

_____

_____

_____

_____

_____

_____

_____

_____

_____

_____

_____

_____

_____

_____

_____

_____

_____

_____

Notes

_____

_____

_____

_____

_____

_____

_____

_____

_____

_____

_____

_____

_____

_____

_____

_____

_____

_____

_____

_____

Chapter 22

"Infamous to Famous"

Imagine the day I received a call to say "Geri Petito you have been nominated for Internet International Hall of Fame for Broadcasting" I almost fell off my chair. Months later I actually did fall off my chair, that call came in December 2019, "Geri Petito, You have been anonymously elected into the Hall of Fame" That same night I was also honored for Host of the Year by my peers. Talk about being humble and grateful to say the least. That same girl that has never been able to shut up was speechless. The best part of that night was when my daughter read the speech she wrote about her mother. I will be sharing with you both her speech and mine from that night. I hope my book can continue to save lives and bring hope to those who need it.

"May the Good Lord Bless and Guide you"

DEC.3, 2019

"My Internet International Hall Of Fame Speech"

TONIGHT I AM EXTREMELY HUMBLED & BEYOND THANKFUL. WHEN I THINK BACK ON MY LIFE I CAN NOT BELIEVE WHERE I AM TODAY. 28 & 1/2 YEARS AGO I GAVE MY LIFE BACK TO CHRIST. I BARGAINED WITH GOD OVER & OVER AGAIN, & WITHOUT FAIL, HE NEVER LEFT ME. SO I FIRST MUST THANK MY LORD & SAVIOR FOR NOT ONLY SAVING MY LIFE, BUT USING ME IN SPITE OF MYSELF. USING MY EXPERIENCES TO HELP OTHERS IN NEED. I WANT TO THANK MY FAMILY & FRIENDS WHO STOOD BY ME & HAD FAITH THAT I WOULD DO MY BEST TO TURN MY LIFE AROUND. ALMOST 4 YEARS AGO, GOD SAID.. WRITE YOUR BOOK, I SMILED & SAID, O.K. WHEN I GOT THE CALL, A WEEK AFTER I SENT IT TO ARCHWAY PUBLISHING, THAT IT WAS GOING TO PRINT, I KNEW GOD HAD MORE FOR ME TO DO. A FEW MONTHS LATER I WAS INTERVIEWED ON HAMILTON RADIO BY D.J. DANI & THEN OFFERED MY OWN SHOW BY DOC G. 3 & 1/2 YEARS AGO WAS MY PREMIERE IN RADIO. HAMILTON RADIO WAS ONE OF THE FIRST NETWORKS TO COMBINE BOTH RADIO & VIDEO. DOC G STARTED THIS, SO I THANK HIM WITH ALL MY HEART. I WANT TO THANK HIS CO OWNERS REUBAN & MONK

FOR ALWAYS MAKING SURE MY SHOWS GO OFF WITHOUT A HITCH!

I WANNA THANK ROB BELL FROM PANJ RADIO FOR MY INTERVIEW ON VINNY'S SHOW. WE SOON BECAME GOOD FRIENDS & STARTED WORKING TOGETHER. I THANK ROB FOR PRODUCING MY SHOWS & DOING AN INCREDIBLE POKER VIDEO OF ME! MY LEAGUE WAS CALLED MsNiteOwlPoker.

ABOUT A YEAR & A HALF AGO I WAS CO HOSTING A SHOW WITH VINCE SCOTT, HIS COUSIN CALLED IN TO SAY HI. NOT KNOWING THIS MAN I WAS MY USUAL CUTE SELF, WHICH LED TO HIM STALKING MY SHOWS! THIS MAN WAS BROTHER O, D.J. OLADSKI. HE REACHED OUT & SAID, GERI PETITO I'D LIKE YOU TO COME ON BOARD AS MY ONLY CAUCASIAN HOST ON BEVERLY NATION. THIS IS WHEN IT JUST GOT REAL!

A SYNDICATED STATION BRINGING ME ON BOARD. BROTHER O'S ABILITY TO MENTOR ME TO THE NEXT LEVEL WAS SURREAL. I HAVE BROKEN 21 RECORDS, & THE FIRST HOST TO BREAK THE HALF MILLION MARK! I THANK BROTHER O FOR BELIEVING IN ME & HIS CONTINUOUS SUPPORT, NOT ONLY TO ME BUT TO ALL HIS HOSTS ON BEVERLY NATION, DAMON NETWORKS & D.A.M.O.N. LOOKS.

I MUST PAY TRIBUTE TO DARLENE LAWRENCE, WHO WAS PART OF THE ORIGINAL BEVERLY

NATION WHO WAS THE FIRST HALL OF FAMER. I NOW WANT TO GIVE A CHEER TO ANDREA PRESLEY, OUR 2ND HALL OF FAMER, UNANIMOUS ELECT. WONDER TWIN WHO ALWAYS GETS IT IN! I LOVE U GIRLFRIEND!

ONTO MY 4TH NETWORK CALLED D.A.M.O.N LOOKS ON YOU TUBE. I THANK BROTHER O FOR HAVING ME AS HIS FIRST HOST ON YOUTUBE. IT IS INCREDIBLE! BEFORE I GO ANY FURTHER I MUST MENTION OUR SISTER ANNA WADDELL. A MEMORY POPPED UP ON FB OF HER MESSAGE TO ME. I WILL NEVER FORGET HER, SHE CALLED ME BEAUTIFUL & TOLD ME SHE LOVED ME. R.I.P. BEAUTIFUL ANGEL.

MY 5TH NETWORK IS REALLY COOL. IT'S CALLED REMEMBER THEN RADIO, RUN BY BARB & STEVE SOSKIN. A SHOUT OUT TO MY GOOD FRIEND MICHAEL D'AMORE, LEAD SINGER OF THE CAPRIS FOR THE INTRO. I THANK U BARB & STEVE FOR BRINGING ME ON BOARD, WHAT A FUN NETWORK, MEETING ALL THE SINGERS FROM THE 50'S & 60'S, SOMEONE PINCH ME PLEASE!

A SHOUT OUT TO OUR "TOWN CRIER" CONGRATULATING OUR CHAMPIONSHIPS, THE ONE & ONLY COMMISSIONER, HUNI BAK ATUN. MAJIK MAN I LOVE YOU MY FRIEND. I WANT TO THANK ALLLL MY FELLOW HOSTS ON ALL MY NETWORKS, WE KEEP EACH OTHER GROUNDED. I WANT

TO THANK ALL MY LISTENERS & VIEWERS. WITHOUT THEM, I WOULD BE TALKING TO MYSELF! I WANT TO THANK MY DAUGHTER TIFFANY FOR ALWAYS STANDING BY ME & TRUSTING IN ME. I AM HONORED THAT YOU ARE SHARING IN THIS NITE WITH ME. I REMEMBER YOU & I DRIVING TOGETHER THAT DAY I GOT THE CALL FROM BROTHER O THAT I WAS NOMINATED. I LOST MY BREATH! I LOVE YOU SO MUCH TIFFANY, I COULDN'T ASK FOR A BETTER DAUGHTER! LAST BUT CERTAINLY NOT LEAST, I WANT TO THANK THE "INTERNET INTERNATIONAL HALL OF FAME" FOR NOT ONLY MY NOMINATION, BUT FOR VOTING ME IN UNANIMOUSLY. FOR BRINGING ME TO THE HIGHEST LEVEL IN BROADCASTING I COULD IMAGINE. I WILL NEVER TAKE THAT FOR GRANTED. I AM HONORED BEYOND WORDS. I THANK YOU FROM THE BOTTOM OF MY HEART!

GERI 😎

To My Mom

Wow! What an accomplishment. In just a few short years, my mom has taken internet radio by storm. She gets the immediate attention of her many listeners with her clever poems and creative ads. And then she draws them in with her unapologetic passion and knowledge. How very proud I am of her. But as proud as I am, I can honestly say I am not surprised. For those of you who haven't realized it by now, my mom is a very strong woman who gets things done. She chose a path in life that many would call the wrong path. But her greatest moment of strength was actually the moment she decided to regain control of her life and overcome that path of addiction. She is who she is today because of THAT path and overcoming it the way she has. She is able to give hope to so many because of THAT path. And it's because of THAT path, that I am here honoring her today. So for those of you who say she chose the "wrong" path, you can stand corrected. There is a reason for everything and God is using my mom and the path she had chosen, to make a difference in the world on a daily basis. The amount of people she has helped through her shows and the book she wrote on addiction is countless, I'm sure.

But the true representation of my mom's heart is shown through the many people she has chosen to successfully help and give her time to. She is Certified Nutritional Health Coach... like that's her job. And you don't know how many times I have had to yell at her because I find out she's not charging people! She's always saying she wants to hit the lottery... but not for the reason that most people want to hit the lottery. She wants to hit the lottery so she could help people. My wife and I are always telling her that if she ever does win the lottery, we would have to be in charge of the money, because she would end up broke, giving it all away, plus some, to everyone else! But seriously though, those are the qualities that I love most about my mom. And I'm so proud to call her my mom and such a loving grandmother to my children. Mom, you deserve this more than anyone I know. Hold your head high, knowing that you have found your purpose in life, and most importantly... that BOTH of your fathers in heaven are so very proud of you. I love you, mom.

TIFFANY

The International Internet Radio
Hall Of Fame

In The Art Of Verbal
Communication Within
Alternative Broadcasting

Geraldine Petito

Hereby Enshrined On This
Day December 3rd 2019

Josef Goldschmidt
Hall Curator

Oladele M Ngozi
C E O G-N-E Syndicated
Stations

CERTIFICATE
Of Achievement

This certificate is presented to :

THE JERSEY JEWEL'
GERI PETITO BY THE
INTERNATIONAL INTERNET
RADIO HALL OF FAME IN PER-
PETUITY FOR OUTSTANDING
PERFORMANCES IN BROAD-
CASTING IN CONTINUANCE TO
SUSTAIN LONGEVITY WITHIN

Josef Goldschmidt Director of
IIRHOF

Signature

ON THIS DAY MARCH
FIFTH, IN THE YEAR
TWO-THOUSAND TH &
NINETEEN

Date

Notes

_____

_____

_____

_____

_____

_____

_____

_____

_____

_____

_____

_____

_____

_____

_____

_____

_____

_____

_____

_____

"My Story Aint Over"

IN TWO THOUSAND SIXTEEN
I PUBLISHED MY BOOK
THE LAST FOUR YEARS
HAVE BEEN OFF THE HOOK!

MY BOOK SIGNINGS WERE GREAT
INTERVIEWED AS WELL
THEN ASKED TO HOST A SHOW
WITH SO MUCH TO TELL

WHO WOULDA THOUGHT
THIS COULD BE TRUE
NOW ON 5 NETWORKS
I'M BROUGHT TO YOU

INTERNATIONAL HALL OF FAME
RADIO SHOW HOST IS ME
SPREADING HOPE ACROSS THE GLOBE
FOR EVERYONE TO SEE

TWENTY-NINE YEARS AGO
MY LIFE WAS A MESS
TWENTY-NINE YEARS LATER
IT'S FILLED WITH SUCCESS!

I NEVER LOST HOPE
I KNEW THERE WAS MORE
I NEEDED TO CHANGE
MY INNER CORE

THE LAST 30 YEARS
MAN...WHAT A RIDE
WHEN I THINK BACK
I WANTED TO HIDE!

I THANK GOD I DIDN'T
HE LED THE WAY
I GAVE HIM MY HAND
I NEEDED TO PRAY

WHAT GOD HAS DONE
FOR ME TO NOW HEAL
HE LED ME TO YOU
TO HELP YOU TO KNEEL

GIVE IT TO GOD
& YOU WON'T REGRET
YOUR LIFE CAN BE CHANGED
YOU DON'T HAVE TO FRET

I'M PROOF...YES I AM
RECOVERY IS REAL
CHANGING YOUR THOUGHTS
WILL ALLOW YOU TO HEAL

GOD MADE ME HIS SERVANT
TO HELP HEAL THE SICK
HARD WORK MUST APPLY
THE FIX...IS NOT QUICK

BUT IF YOU DO WANT IT
HARD WORK WILL PREVAIL
FROM...A ONE TO A TEN
YOU'LL REACH THE SCALE!

A NUTRITIONAL HEALTH COACH
A RECOVERY COACH TOO
GOD PUT ME HERE
TO REALLY HELP YOU

I'LL NEVER STOP TRYING
'TILL GOD SAYS ENOUGH
HE'S SHOWN ME MY JOURNEY
HE MADE ME REAL TOUGH

PROUD OF MY CERTIFICATES
THEY ALL STATE MY NAME
I DISPLAY THEM WITH PRIDE
ON MY WALL OF FAME!

NOW TWENTY TWENTY
REVISED...IS MY BOOK
THE LAST FOUR YEARS
HAVE BEEN OFF THE HOOK!

Geri Petito

"COVID-19"

2020 STARTED WITH A BANG
NOT IN A GOOD WAY THOUGH
A VIRUS CALLED CORONA CAME
FOR ALL THE WORLD TO KNOW

"COVID-19"
IS THE REAL NAME
THIS VIRUS IS DEADLY
IT BROUGHT WORLD FAME!

A PANDEMIC HAUNTING NATIONS
SOMETHING STRANGE TO ME
NEVER IN MY LIFETIME
THOUGHT I'D EVER SEE!

STREETS ARE EMPTY
SUPPLIES ARE SCARCE
FEAR IS ON THE RISE
THE CALM'S NOW FIERCE!

BUSINESSES ARE CLOSING
PEOPLE OUT OF WORK
WITHOUT HAPPY MOMENTS
DOOM AND GLOOM NOW LURK

CURFEWS ARE INSTILLED
TO ONLY BUY SOME FOOD
ALL THIS SCARY NEWS
DESTROYS & HURTS OUR MOOD

BEING ON LOCK DOWN
IS SOMETHING FAR FETCHED
IS THIS STUFF REALLY REAL
OUR THOUGHTS ARE STRETCHED!

ESSENTIAL WORKERS ONLY
ARE WORKING LONG NIGHTS
TRYING TO HELP OUT
AT ALL NEEDED SITES!

HOSPITAL WORKERS & PHARMACISTS
GROCERY STORES & BANKS
SANITATION WORKERS & TEACHERS
ARE NOW THE ONES WITH RANKS

EMT'S & POLICEMEN
ARE ALSO SERVING US
DURING STORMY WEATHER
WE KNOW WHO WE SHOULD TRUST

THIS VIRUS CAME WITH FORCE
IN A MINUTE, IT WAS HERE
IT STARTED OUT IN CHINA
WITH NO SIGNS, TO DISAPPEAR

WE CAN'T SEE OUR FAMILIES
QUARANTINED AT HOME
CAN NOT GO OUTSIDE
OUR KIDS & PETS, CAN'T ROAM

Geri Petito

THEY'RE CLOSING ALL STATE PARKS
SIX FEET APART WE MUST STAND
HOW COULD THIS HAVE HAPPENED
BY THE GOVERNMENTS COMMAND

THE LAND OF THE FREE
THE HOME OF THE BRAVE
WAS WHO WE ONCE WERE...
NOW WE FEEL CONTROLLED
COMMUNISM WILL STIR

ALL APPOINTMENTS CANCELLED
STIR CRAZY MOST HAVE GONE
IF THERE IS A LIGHT TO SHINE
PLEASE SOMEONE TURN IT ON

WE CAN NOT HUG OUR FRIENDS
ALL GATHERINGS ARE CLOSED
WE WERE MADE TO BE SOCIAL
VULNERABILITY'S EXPOSED

MAN CAN NOT LIVE
ON BEING ALONE
THROUGH THIS CONFINEMENT
HIS HEART'S BEING SHOWN

I HOPE THROUGH THIS CRISIS
WE ALL FINALLY SEE
HOW LIFE SHOULD BE LIVED
THAT LOVE IS THE KEY!

PEOPLE ARE DYEING
I'VE LOST SOME TOO
NOW EVEN ANIMALS
LOCKED IN A ZOO

I DON'T REALLY SEE
AN END IN NEAR SIGHT
NOT HERE ON EARTH
IN HEAVEN, THAT'S RIGHT

I BELIEVE IT'S A WARNING
THAT GOD'S HAD ENOUGH
REVELATIONS FORETOLD IT
IT TELLS YOU THIS STUFF!

AS PROPHECY UNFOLDS
YOU CAN'T RUN & HIDE
JESUS IS BEGGING YOU
TO RUN TO HIS SIDE

THERE'S BEEN SO MUCH EVIL
FROM MAN ON THIS EARTH
SATAN'S BEEN RULING
& CURSING GOD'S WORTH!

THE SIGNS ARE ALL THERE
I BEG YOU TO LISTEN
NOW IS THE TIME TO
PUT CHRIST IN YOUR VISION

GOD IS NOT PLAYING
THE TIME IS NOW HERE
GOD'S WRATH IS UPON US
TAKE UP YOUR SPEAR

IF THE END TIMES ARE NOW
I'M WARNING YOU THIS
YOU BETTER BE READY
DON'T BE REMISS

I DON'T CARE HOW THIS STARTED
I'M HERE TO BRING YOU HOPE
DON'T SAY THERE IS NO GOD
'CAUSE HE CAN HELP YOU COPE

THE GOVERNMENT & SATAN
WILL TRY TO BREAK US DOWN
KEEP YOUR EYES ON JESUS
HIS TRUTH, IT SHOULD BE FOUND!

THE BIBLE IS UNFOLDING
IT'S HAPPENING RIGHT NOW
I BEG YOU ALL, TO TAKE A KNEE
PRAY TO GOD, TO SAVE YOU NOW!

GOD HELP US ALL
I ASK FOR FORGIVENESS
PLEASE HEAL THIS WORLD
THROUGH ALL OF THIS STILLNESS!

GERI

"I HEAR YOU, NOW HEAR ME"

I HEAR YOU
NOW HEAR ME
OPEN OUR EYES
SO WE CAN SEE

AN ARTIST BY TRADE
ALL COLORS I SEE
ALL ARE SO PRETTY
TO SOMEONE LIKE ME

PEOPLE OF COLOR
I WANT YOU TO KNOW
HOW MOST OF US THINK
SO HERE I GO...

BECAUSE OF OUR AGES
ONLY KNOW WHAT'S BEEN TOLD
WE WERE TAUGHT IN SCHOOL
THE LIES THAT THEY SOLD!

HISTORY IS HISTORY
I DON'T UNDERSTAND
TAUGHT DIFFERENTLY
DEPENDING ON MAN

WE CAN'T CHANGE THE PAST
WE WEREN'T TO BLAME
OUR FOREFATHERS IN CHARGE
ON THEM, IS THE SHAME

Geri Petito

IF YOU LIVE IN THE NORTH
OR LIVE IN THE SOUTH
CONFLICTS ON HISTORY
BY WORD OF MOUTH

WE'RE ALL TAUGHT LIES
BACK THEN & NOW
PEOPLE OF COLOR
THIS IS HOW...

WHITE PEOPLE WE'RE TOLD
COLUMBUS WAS GREAT
'TILL I MET TRUE NATIVES
WHO SET ME STRAIGHT!

ARE YOU KIDDING ME
HE MURDERED YOU
HE RAPED & STOLE
YOUR KIDS TOO

TO THIS VERY DAY
STILL HAVE FEW RIGHTS
RIPPED AT THEIR CORE
BY MOSTLY "WHITES"

THE HOLOCAUST
NOT TO FAR BACK
MY PARENTS LIFETIME
WAS THIS ATTACK

JEWISH PEOPLE
TORTURED AND KILLED
THEY STARTED OVER
TO THEN REBUILD

THE 17th & 18th CENTURIES
FROM AFRICA PEOPLE WERE SOLD
BROUGHT TO THE US
NOT HUMAN, THEY WERE TOLD

THE WHITE MAN USED & ABUSED
OWNED & TRADED THEIR LIVES
THEIR RIGHTS WERE TAKEN AWAY
STORIES FOUND IN ARCHIVES

I HEAR YOU
NOW PLEASE HEAR ME
13th AMMENDMENT IN 1865
MADE TO SET YOU FREE

WE WERE TAUGHT
& YES, MISLED
TO NOW BELIEVE
SLAVERY IS DEAD

I HEAR YOU
NOW PLEASE HEAR ME
MOST OF US TODAY
NO COLOR, WE SEE

YES, THERE'S RACISTS
& VERY, VERY BAD "MEN"
UNDERSTAND, WE CAN NOT
REPEAT HISTORY AGAIN

EVEN 4th OF JULY
WHICH WE NEVER KNEW
CELEBRATING INDEPENDENCE
FROM BRITISH RULE

WHILE WE FOUGHT FREEDOM
JUST FOR THE WHITES?
BLACKS WERE ENSLAVED
STRIPPED OF THEIR RIGHTS!

HOW HYPOCRITICAL
THIS SEEMS TO ME
HOW DID THIS HAPPEN
HOW COULD THIS BE?!

I HEAR YOU
NOW HEAR ME
I DID RESEARCH
SO I COULD SEE

I ALMOST SAID SCREW IT
WON'T CELEBRATE AGAIN
BUT REALIZED THE DATE
WE STARTED BACK THEN

A FEDERAL HOLIDAY IT BECAME
IN NINETEEN FORTY ONE
I DO FEEL BETTER KNOWING THIS
BUT STILL, OUR WORKS NOT DONE!

I HEAR YOU
NOW HEAR ME
I HAVE THE ANSWER
WE NEED TO SEE

PEOPLE OF COLOR
I'M NOT TO BLAME
PEOPLE OF COLOR
THIS I CLAIM!!

I HEAR YOU
NOW PLEASE HEAR ME
WE WANNA LISTEN
IN PEACE, IT SHOULD BE

WE WEREN'T THE ONES
WHO STARTED THIS MESS
WE'RE WILLING TO HELP
TO BRING YOU SUCCESS

I HEAR YOU
NOW PLEASE HEAR ME
WHEN YOU ATTACK YOUR OWN
VIOLENCE WE SEE

I HEAR YOU
NOW PLEASE HEAR ME
LET YOUR VOICE BE HEARD
YES, IT NEEDS TO BE

RIOTS & TARGETING
ANYONE IN SIGHT
MAKES YOU WRONG
WON'T MAKE YOU RIGHT

IF YOU PROTEST IN PEACE
LIKE MARTIN LUTHER DID
1968 HE DIED
PROTESTING WHAT THEY DID

OVER FIFTY YEARS AGO
MARTIN SET THE STAGE
TO STOP ALL THE VIOLENCE
LET PEACEFUL ACTS ENGAGE

I HEAR YOU
NOW PLEASE HEAR ME
I THINK THE WORLD IS READY...
IF YOU TRULY WANT TO BE HEARD
PROTEST WITH PEACE , FAST & STEADY!

YES, IT'S TIME
THE LIES ARE KILLED
THE TRUTH MUST NOW PREVAIL...
THE WAY TO OPEN UP OUR EYES
MARCH FORTH IN PEACE TO NO AVAIL!

DOES RACISM STILL EXIST
UNFORTUNATELY IT DOES
BUT THOSE IGNORANT PEOPLE
DON'T REPRESENT MOST OF US!

I'D BE THE FIRST TO MARCH WITH YOU
MY GRAND DAUGHTER IS PART BLACK
BUT ONLY IF IT'S PEACEFUL & CALM
IN LOVE, I WOULD HAVE YOUR BACK!

ARE THERE BAD COPS
OH, HELL YEAH
BUT MOST IN BLUE
THEY DO CARE

YOUR ANGER IS TARGETED
AT MOST AS A WHOLE
THAT IS SO UNFAIR
IT RIPS AT YOUR SOLE

IT'S TIME NOW
WE COME TOGETHER
BEFORE IT IS TO LATE...
IT'S TIME NOW
WE WALK IN LOVE
BEFORE WE REACH THAT GATE

GOD IS REAL, I KID YOU NOT
HIS VOICE IS BEING HEARD...
PLEASE TAKE HEED, & LISTEN
END TIMES, IS IN THE WORD

HE DIED FOR ME, HE DIED FOR YOU
ALL COLORS MATTER, THAT'S RIGHT
JESUS CHRIST THE MAN HIMSELF
PORTRAYED AS, BUT WASN'T WHITE!

I HEAR YOU
NOW HEAR ME
BLACK LIVES MATTER
BUT SO DO WE

BLUE LIVES MATTER
OH YES THEY DO
WITHOUT THEM
WE'RE DOOMED TOO

NOW IT'S TIME
WE DO UNITE
TAKE THOSE WRONGS
& MAKE THEM RIGHT!

GERI

Amazing Book Reviews

Judy Ortado

5.0 out of 5 stars <u>A must read!!!</u>
Reviewed in the United States on January 12, 2019
<u>Format: Paperback</u>
I read this book before I had the unique pleasure of meeting Geri. I was literally awestruck by her honesty and candor. This book is a soul-searching confessional, written with humor and a light hearted edge. It is a bible for those who struggle with addiction and a wake up call for those who fail to strive for optimism when faced with adversity. Please do not let this book slip through your fingers. It is a rare find. God bless you, Geri!

T. O.

5.0 out of 5 stars <u>Please read this book, it may just save someone's life</u>
Reviewed in the United States on February 17, 2019
<u>Format: Paperback</u>
This book has opened my eyes to realize even being clean over 4 years that I must stay on top of my recovery. Geri is brutally honest in her book and touches on things I can relate to first hand. It let's us know that we can change no matter how dark a road you are going down. I really enjoyed reading her book and I definitely recommend this to all recovering addicts and to the addict that still suffers today. I will be mentioning this book at my next therapy session as a unique tool everyone can use on their road to recovery... Thank you Geri for sharing your story with us.

Amazon Customer

5.0 out of 5 stars <u>How to deal with an addiction.</u>
Reviewed in the United States on June 25, 2018
Format: Kindle Edition
This is the best advice I have seen in writing. I am sure the writer saved many lives from this unique way of writing and handling this terrible addiction. This book comes from deep in the heart and soul of the writer. I

am the oldest of six, two having the addiction very bad. I lost one because as you said I was enabling him. By time I got to the younger one, I did what you said and found tough love. She made it like yourself. Its so great to see the pen that is mightier than the sword on paper as you wrote this. I am sure God has gifted you in so many ways and I am thankful you are out there giving such good advise in this book. I know it works which I can vision clearly. I enjoyed reading this strong book of great messages. Gob Bless you Geri Petito.

LENNY VENITO

5.0 out of 5 stars <u>I enjoyed reading this book</u>
Reviewed in the United States on June 2, 2016
Format: PaperbackVerified Purchase
I enjoyed reading this book. The author, writing from personal experience, clearly gives a persuasive argument for the thinking that addiction is a choice and not a decease. Yes it is mental dependence but not a decease. She gives insight into what it is like to be an addict and try to quit. Not easy but, do-able. I can not help but agree with her on the fact that although an addict needs the support of family and some kind of counselling, organized groups like AA and NA only help to keep the addict in a state of perpetual addition by reinforcing the notion that you are recovering for the rest of your life and can never be considered not an addict. Ms. Petito provides a simple course of action

with simple, plain English writing. The book is not a novel, it is only 47 pages long. Anyone, even with a short span of attention can read it and understand it. If you are an addict or know someone who is and want to find help. BUY THIS BOOK!..READ THIS BOOK!.. Thank You Ms. Petito.

new jersey

5.0 out of 5 stars An addiction free life
Reviewed in the United States on May 30, 2016
Format: PaperbackVerified Purchase
Geri gives you down to earth guidance for dealing with addictions. She inspires the reader at the beginning of each chapter with a short poem. It is obvious that Geri wants her readers to search their souls and realize that they can have a better life. It is a short, direct to the point book, on starting down a new and exciting path. An addiction free life.
One person found this helpful

5.0 out of 5 stars I loved this book
Reviewed in the United States on May 27, 2016
Format: Kindle Edition
I loved this book! It was funny and interesting. I love how there was a pome at the start of every chapter.

I found Geri to be real and I love her no nonsense approach to healing yourself, not of the "disease" of addiction, but the choice you make to poison yourself. I'm sure this book will help many people looking for answers.

3 people found this helpful

Amazon Customer

5.0 out of 5 stars The best book I have ever read
Reviewed in the United States on May 29, 2016
Format: PaperbackVerified Purchase
The best book I have ever read!!! If you are someone you know are an addict or recovering addict, You MUST get this book. It is life changing!!!

5.0 out of 5 stars Fantastic Book !!!!
Reviewed in the United States on June 28, 2016
Format: Paperback
This book is fantastic. It was given to me by a friend who thought that it may be helpful to me. This book has helped me tremendously. It can help with ANY sort of addiction a person may struggle with. My particular issue is food addiction. The author, Geri Petito, gives her honest account of an earlier drug addiction and the journey she decided to take to change her life and her

choices which led to her now having a fantastic, healthy and happy life. She provides from-the-heart advice on how to overcome addiction of any sort with honesty, humor and solid recommendations that really work for those who honestly desire to change the direction of their life and move forward once and for all. I read this book quickly and could not wait to turn the next page. I've already read it several times because it gives me the "reinforcements" I need to continue my journey. I've since purchased three more copies of it to give to friends that could absolutely benefit from it. This book will make you laugh and it will make you cry, but most importantly it will make you CHANGE !!!

One person found this helpful

5.0 out of 5 stars <u>Great read.</u>
Reviewed in the United States on June 2, 2016
Format: PaperbackVerified Purchase
Amazing story of an incredible journey.
One person found this helpful

Kindle Customer

5.0 out of 5 stars <u>Five Stars</u>
Reviewed in the United States on June 13, 2016
Format: PaperbackVerified Purchase
Excellent read, love it and am sharing with family!
One person found this helpful

<u>Cheyenne Rhodes</u>

January 31 at 5:32 PM ·
Just finished this amazing book. Thank you <u>Geri Petito</u>
for having the courage to put yourself, your beliefs and
your words out there. The pen is a mighty tool when

coupled with a beautiful mind ♥.

October,3 2019
Hey Geri I just finished your book, in fact I'd read it 1.5
times. I had to re-read the 2nd half of it just because it
was so real, honest, and true. I myself am a victim and
veteran of the arts and how this crazy world measures
success based on sales and attendances...long story short
your book is on the level of Wild At Heart and the many
other billllllllion-zillllllllion selling books. If only we could

burn ever Joel Osteen books and replace it with "I'm Not an Addict... I'm Just an Ass!"... If only other female (and male) recovery coaches not only admitted the existence of Jesus tHey Geri I just finished your book, in fact I'd read it 1.5 times. I had to re-read the 2nd half of it just because it was so real, honest, and true. I myself am a victim and veteran of the arts and how this crazy world measures success based on sales and attendances...long story short your book is on the level of Wild At Heart and the many other billlllllllion-zilllllllllion selling books. If only we could burn ever Joel Osteen books and replace it with "I'm Not an Addict... I'm Just an Ass!"... If only other female (and male) recovery coaches not only admitted the existence of Jesus the Christ but also pointed out the fact that Jesus was not religious (for religion is poison) but to believe in Him IS NOT religious. A relationship with Jesus Christ is so important that not only our schools but also our churches have "evolved" into organizations that teach and preach anything other than what He lived and died for. Love! That being said, I loved your book! The world needs more fearless humility such as yours. If you're free tomorrow shoot me a call, I'd love to talk to you. God bless... he Christ but also pointed out the fact that Jesus was not religious (for religion is poison) but to believe in Him IS NOT religious. A relationship with Jesus Christ is so important that not only our schools but also our churches have "evolved" into organizations that teach and preach anything other than what He lived and died for. Love! That being said, I loved your book! The world needs more fearless humility such as your, I'd love to talk to you. God bless. Chris

February 2, 2020

I met Geri a few years back at my Radio Show where she was gracious enough to donate her book. I have to admit I chuckled at the name of the book and thought how could this possibly help someone with their addictions, I read the book and realized this woman was what you see is what you get and she speaks the harsh truth and I got it. Her spirituality helped her not only get through her addictions, also helped so many along the way. Her poetic way of expressing her journey is a must read for anyone – Not just an Ass…lol who would of thought 4 years later I'd be the one helping her revise her book… **Jusella Bella**

 Mitchell Frederick Koons — with **Geri Petito**.
Jan 29, 2017 at 8:52 PM ·

My #1 when I need someone to talk with. **Geri Petito** has helped me through some of the worst situations i have been in my life. I only want to thank her for all of her support and even including Ms Nite owl Poker. The league that I played in with such great people she had brought into my life. Thanks again for making me believe I am not an addict, but just an ass.

This book goes most places I do, it fits in my back pocket. It's truly a self help book speaking very bluntly with lovely poems and references from personal experience.

 Geri Petito
Jan 28, 2017 at 9:03 PM ·

HEY GUYS…MY VIDEO IS READY!! PLEASE SHARE YOUR BUTTS OFF…THANX!! U ALLL OWE ME! LOL

Maria Rose is with **Geri Petito**.

Feb 16, 2018 at 3:53 PM · 🌐

Today I read this book from cover to cover, and honestly it opened my eyes to new ways of thinking. This book has taught me that everyone has choices in life. No one else controls what you do in your life but you. Making changes in your life isn't something you half-ass (no pun intended 😂😂😂), it's all or nothing. Above all, it's taught me that despite circumstance, I can live a happy life.

A big thank you to the author of this book, my friend Geri Petito. Thank you for love, your light, and support through everything. I'm truly blessed to have someone like you in my life. Your words have impacted my life more than you can even fathom. Hugs mama 😊😊😊

And btw - I HIGHLY recommend this book. It can help anyone struggling through life, not just those going through addiction

Printed in the United States
By Bookmasters